TIME FOR ASSEMBLY

TIME FOR ASSEMBLY

Assemblies for 8-12s
with optional follow-up
work for the class-room

ANNE FARNCOMBE

NATIONAL CHRISTIAN EDUCATION COUNCIL

Robert Denholm House
Nutfield, Redhill, Surrey, RH1 4HW

To ANNE and BILL

First published 1980
© Anne Farncombe

0 7197 0263 1

Typeset by Graphics 2000 Limited, Dorking, Surrey
Printed and bound by Staples Printers Rochester Ltd, Kent

Contents

Introduction

Time for Assembly is published in response to the request of many teachers in Middle schools for a book containing *all* the material required for Assemblies. This book provides that material — talks and stories, prayers, poems, and Bible readings, with suggestions for hymns, both traditional and modern. For some Assemblies music is suggested, which could be played at the beginning of the Assembly to create an atmosphere related to the theme, during the Assembly, or at the end, as appropriate.

For those teachers who want to continue the theme of the Assembly in the class-room, follow-up work is provided. In a few instances this could lead to a further Assembly led by the children.

Most of the hymns and songs suggested are well known and may be found in standard hymn books. Less well-known songs have been selected from two books in common use in Middle schools: *Come and Praise* (BBC), and *Sing it in the Morning* (Nelson).

A world to discover

The Assembly

Preparation
Have ready a tray with a lump of coal on it, covered with a cloth.

Talk and story
Here is a tray, covered with a cloth. Underneath the cloth is a valuable object. *(Choose a child to take away the cloth.)* He has UNcovered the precious object. What is it? Would you call it precious or valuable? Where does it come from?

Millions and millions of years ago a tall tree stood with its roots in soft, swampy ground. Its top branches swayed in the sun and its feathery leaves rustled in the wind. It was a proud tree. 'I will live for ever,' it murmured among the other forest plants, who shook themselves knowingly. But the tall tree lost its strength; the bottom of its trunk rotted in the warm, swampy water and, one day, as the wind whistled down from the hills, it overbalanced. Crash! The whole forest shook. The delicate ferns trembled long after the tree trunk became still, and the swamp water rippled and sighed for days.

Many years later the whole forest had gone. The ferns and swaying plants had sunk into the swamp, the tree trunks and thick branches had crumbled, and the whole area had become a mass of rotted vegetation. Heat rose in little swirls of steam from the sodden ground. The proud tree and the beautiful forest had disappeared. Sometimes the earth rumbled and moved, and the rotten vegetation sank lower, covered with layers of mud and sand and rocks.

But the proud tree was turning into something valuable within the earth. Heat from below and pressure from above gradually dried it, along with all the other forest trees, until it became hard and rock-like.

Millions of years later man began to UNcover the earth; off came layer upon layer of rock and soil until the moment, when, deep, deep down, the hard black rock was found. Not only was it UNcovered, it was DIScovered. Man held the black glossy rock in his hands. No one really knows how he came to use it as a fuel; perhaps he tried to use it as a tool, but it was too brittle; perhaps he tried to use it to scrape down the sides of his cave and found it left

7

dirty black marks; perhaps he threw it onto his wood fire in disgust, thinking it was no good for anything. At any rate, he soon discovered that it would burn longer and with greater heat than wood, and he began to dig more and more of it out of its secret place under the earth.

The proud forest tree had not died after all; for thousands of years it, and others like it, would be of use to man.

Look at this lump of coal; you are looking at something which is probably older than anything else you will see in your lifetime. Look at the world, God's world. UNcover it with your eyes, but DIScover it with your curiosity. God has given you all the treasures of the earth — go and look for them.

Readings
Listen to some verses from one of the great songs of the Bible:

Praise the Lord, my soul!
You have set the earth firmly on its foundations,
    and it will never be moved.
You placed the ocean over it like a robe,
    and the water covered the mountains.
You make springs flow in the valleys,
    and rivers run between the hills.
They provide water for the wild animals;
    there the wild donkeys quench their thirst.
In the trees near by,
    the birds make their nests and sing.
The cedars of Lebanon get plenty of rain —
    the Lord's own trees, which he planted.
There the birds build their nests;
    the storks nest in the fir-trees.
The wild goats live in the high mountains,
    and the badgers hide in the cliffs.
Praise the Lord, my soul!
Praise the Lord.

(Psalm 104.1a,5-6,10-12,16-18,35b, GNB)

Isaiah, one of the prophets who gave strength to the people of Israel, said:

As the waters fill the sea, so shall the land be filled with the knowledge of the Lord.

(Isaiah 11.9, NEB)

8

Hymns
All things bright and beautiful
For the beauty of the earth
When the world is dark and dreary   (SM 54)

Prayer
O God, help us to do more than simply drift through your world seeing only
the surface of things. May every day be one of excitement and discovery as we
wonder at your world around us. So may our wonder turn to praise, and our
praise become part of our worship.

Music
Beethoven: Symphony No 6 (Pastoral) — opening of slow movement.
Song: Wonderful world.

Follow-up for the class-room

1   Make a display table of the uses of coal: soap, plastics, gas, perfume,
antiseptics, nylon, washing powders, aspirins, etc.

2   Discover how coal is mined, making sectional drawings of a mine,
showing the layers of earth and rock through which the shafts are cut.

3   Experiment with coal. Will it dissolve? Is it porous? Can you draw with it?
How would you grind it down to powder? What does it look like through a
magnifying glass or a microscope?

4   Set simple tasks of discovery.
Water: In humans, plants and animals; water for heating, for drinking;
experiments in filtering river, stream or sea water. Microscopic examination
of life in a drop of water. Rain, steam, snow, cloud, etc.
Pattern all round us: Brick walls, corrugated iron, tiles on roofs, repeated
patterns on fabrics and wallpaper; patterns that are created by texture;
patterns used as camouflage, etc.
Curiosity and inventiveness: How one often leads to another. Man learning to use
God's gifts by trial and error, to provide himself with food, clothing, warmth
and light.
Need and inventiveness: Man's desire to make a better, safer world. Discoveries

9

of cures for, and prevention of, disease; the harness of electricity; the use of oil; building materials, etc.

5   Men and women who made discoveries in God's world: Nansen, Scott, Lister, Marie Curie, Ronald Ross, etc.

Additional story: Mosquito Ross
Dr Ronald Ross stood looking down at his patient. The little Indian boy was shivering violently, but was sticky with sweat. His mother wiped his face with a damp rag, no longer cool and clean. Insects droned and buzzed in the little hut, settling here and there in silence, then flying on through the air with a monotonous whine.

Dr Ross shook his head. The boy had fallen into an uneasy sleep, turning and moaning, and the doctor stooped through the doorway into the fresh air. He knew that next time he called the boy would be dead; he had seen it so often before. Many people died from this dreadful disease called *bad-air* or *mal-aria*. Perhaps he would be sent for soon to attend the boy's mother, or his brothers and sisters, as the disease took hold of them, too. It spread so quickly here in India; he knew, too, that it was costing thousands of lives in other tropical countries throughout the world.

The doctor brushed a mosquito from his face. The air was misty with these little insects, especially near the village well and by the swampy water-holes on the edge of the forest. People believed that malaria came from the bad air round the waters and swamps, and drank as little as possible. He had heard people say that if you drank water that had a small mosquito grub in it you would be sure to die from the disease. Perhaps if they emptied all the water away the disease would go.

But another idea was forming in the doctor's head. Supposing it was the insect itself that was spreading the disease, in its bite? That year, he spent most of his leave in England studying tropical insects. His friends even gave him the nickname 'Mosquito Ross' and laughed at him, but he would not give up. 'If I can discover the cause of the spread of malaria,' he thought, 'then we can begin to fight it effectively.'

Back in India, almost suffocating with the heat in his room, Ronald Ross worked with his microscope. He took samples of blood from patients suffering from malaria, and looked at them closely until he could identify the germs responsible for the disease. He also caught hundreds of mosquitoes to see whether he could discover the same germs on, or in, them. It was a long and difficult job because there were many different kinds of mosquito.

At last, late one night, he examined a new kind of mosquito — and the germs it carried were the same as those on his blood samples! He knew he had discovered how malaria was spread. This particular kind of mosquito bit

10

someone who had malaria, sucking out some of his blood, and then went on to bite a healthy person, leaving a deposit of the infected blood. Dr Ross was happy in his discovery.

Twenty years passed, however, before he was believed. During those twenty frustrating years Dr Ronald Ross fought malaria on his own. Everywhere he went he spent much of his time making sure that the dreaded insects could not breed in uncovered water, and wherever he destroyed the mosquitoes the disease disappeared.

At last he proved that his theory was right, and a new hospital was set up in London called the *Ross Institute and Hospital for Tropical Diseases.*

Today, perhaps at this very minute, a small plane swoops low over the swamps of India leaving behind it clouds of poison that falls and settles, killing the mosquitoes. More planes are doing the same in Africa and South America. The World Health Organisation is continuing the fight that Dr Ronald Ross began.

Promises, promises

The Assembly

Story

Mary and Mark were getting ready for school. 'Where are my clean socks?' Mark shouted down the stairs. 'Can I have bacon sandwiches in my lunch box today?' Mary called.

Mother was in a hurry this morning. She had called the children early, and made sure they washed, then hurried down to begin getting the breakfast ready. Father was cutting sandwiches for the lunch boxes at the same time as keeping an eye on the toast, while the cat asked to be let out, and the kettle boiled furiously. At last the children came down, ready to eat their breakfast. Mark wasn't quite able to get his school tie right, and Mary was convinced that her school homework book was lost, but it was surprising how quickly these things were put right by Mother and Father.

'You'll have to start a bit early for school this morning,' Father said as they finished breakfast. 'I shan't be able to take you by car today. Mother and I have promised to be at Grandma's house by half-past eight, and we can't let her down. But you've walked before, so you should be all right if you're careful.'

Mary liked walking to school. Her friends often went the same way and then they all arrived at the school gate together. Mark wasn't quite so happy.

'I don't like walking,' he said, 'and Mary always goes so quickly.'

'Now, Mary,' said Mother, as they all buttoned up their coats, 'will you make me a promise?'

'Of course,' said Mary.

'Promise to hold Mark's hand all the way,' Mother said. 'And remember he's much younger than you.'

'All right,' agreed Mary, as she and Mark set off down the garden path together. 'Now hold my hand,' she said, as they turned right along the pavement. Mark put his hand in hers, and they hurried along so that they would not be late.

'Mind the road,' warned Mary, as they turned a corner.

'Mary!' shouted someone from the opposite pavement. It was Judy, Mary's friend. Mary dropped Mark's hand to wave.

'Wait for me!' she called, and ran across the road to where Judy was standing. Mark was left on the other side. He hesitated for a moment, then ran out to cross the road — straight into a bicycle that was being ridden round the corner!

Mary heard him scream, and she heard the bump and crash as the bicycle fell over. She turned quickly, cold with fright. Mark was lying in the road with the bicycle on top of him. The cyclist sat for a moment in a daze, then began to lift his bike off Mark. Mary was there, too, brushing Mark down as he struggled to stand up.

'I'm all right,' he said. But a teacher who was passing in his car at that moment insisted on taking him to the hospital to be checked by a doctor.

Mother hurried to the hospital from Grandma's house when they telephoned her. The doctor was reassuring: 'He's only got a few bruises,' he said. 'He's had a bit of a shock, though. Take him home and keep him warm today. In a few days he'll be as right as rain.'

'It could have been much worse,' said Mother. She guessed what had happened, and looked at Mary sadly.

Mary felt terrible. She had broken her promise. She had let her mother down, and she had allowed her little brother to run into danger.

Could Mother ever trust Mary to take Mark to school again?

Reading

Jesus once told a story about people who let someone down:

'A man was giving a big dinner party and had sent out many invitations. At dinner-time he sent his servant with a message for his guests, "Please come, everything is now ready." They began one and all to excuse themselves. The first said, "I have bought a piece of land, and I must go and look over it; please accept my apologies." The second said, "I have bought five yoke of oxen, and I am on my way to try them out; please accept my apologies." The next said, "I have just got married and for that reason I cannot come." When the servant came back he reported this to his master. The master of the house was angry and said to him, "Go out quickly into the streets and alleys of the town, and bring me in the poor, the crippled, the blind, and the lame." The servant said, "Sir, your orders have been carried out and there is still room." The master replied, "Go out on to the highways and along the hedgerows and make them come in; I want my house to be full." '

(Luke 14.16-23, NEB)

13

Hymns
Can you be sure that the rain will fall?   (CP 31)
Jesus, good above all other
O Jesus, I have promised

Prayer
Help us, O God, to be people who can be trusted. When we make promises, make us strong enough to keep them. May we always be careful in what we say and what we do, so that others will know that they can rely on us. May we learn to have confidence in you, trusting in your promises, and knowing that you will never let us down.

Follow-up for the class-room

1   Those who belong to uniformed organisations (or other organisations if appropriate) could tell the class about the promises they have to make to be accepted as full members. Encourage a discussion of times when they have (a) forgotten the promise, (b) carelessly or deliberately broken it, or (c) kept it, even though it has meant inconvenience or hardship.

2   Examine how we trust others to keep their promises to us, eg the Bank of England to honour the promise on a pound note; services such as electricity and gas boards to supply us constantly with power or fuel. The children will be able to make further suggestions of people or groups of people whom they trust without question. What would happen if their promises, explicit or implied, were not kept?

3   Get the children to work out this message, which can be written in two lines on the blackboard:

I	Y	U	E	P	O	R	R	M	S	Y	U	I	L	E	R	S	E
F	O	K	E	Y	U	P	O	I	E	O	W	L	B	T	U	T	D

4   Read together Rudyard Kipling's poem *The Explorer*.

5   Tell the children the story of Abraham: how God had promised that one day he would become the father of a great nation. Abraham trusted God's

14

promise, and set out on a long and dangerous journey into the unknown: Genesis 12.1-10; 13.1-4. Draw a picture map of this journey, and quote Paul's words about Abraham: 'He was absolutely sure that God would be able to do what he had promised.' *(Romans 4.21, GNB)*

In someone else's shoes

The Assembly

Story: Shortie Stewart and his new shoes

Robert could see Stewart's new shoes. He was pretending not to look too interested, or envious, because he didn't like Stewart; but really the new shoes were something! Just the sort he'd been trying to persuade Dad to buy him for ages. When they changed for football, Stewart saw Robert staring at the shoes.

'Want to try them on?' he asked.

'No fear,' said Robert, 'they're awful!'

Stewart turned away, his face red and his glasses steamed up. Someone pushed him aside.

'Out of the way, Shortie Stewart! And take those stupid glasses off when you're on the football pitch, you'll only break them.'

It was a good game, rough and tough, and Robert's team won again. The other team didn't stand a chance while old four-eyes, Shortie Stewart, was in it.

Late that night, Robert had a dream. He rather liked dreams, for there was nearly always adventure, and sometimes a bit of real daring, in them. In this dream, Stewart's shoes were by Robert's table at school. The room was empty, and Robert couldn't resist trying them on. Very comfortable they were, and smart and modern. Robert paraded up and down between the rows of tables. Suddenly the door burst open, and all his friends came in, Big Bob, and Mike the Pike, and old Frenchy.

'Playtime!' they shouted.

'I've got a ball, give you a kick, Frenchy,' said Mike.

'Wait for me,' Robert urged, trying to kick off Stewart's new shoes. But they were suddenly too tight to budge.

'Oh no, Shortie Stewart, you stay where you are, we don't want you!' he heard someone say. Robert gasped. Perhaps they thought he really was Stewart, just because he was wearing his shoes.

'Wait a minute, fellows,' he protested. His voice came out with a thin, high-pitched sound — goodness, he even sounded like Stewart! He went to rub his eyes and his hands touched — spectacles! Oh no. He stumbled out of the room and followed his friends into the playground.

16

'Get out of our game!' shouted Big Bob, as Robert tried to field the ball. 'Go off on your own, Shortie Stewart!'

Robert shuffled off miserably. Everyone else suddenly seemed much bigger and stronger than he was, and no one took any notice as he stood alone by the playground wall. His glasses were misty. He took them off to clean them, and suddenly everything was blurred. He blinked hard, but the children in the playground looked like a frightening mass of moving, screaming, unknown people. When he put his glasses on again he could see them all, laughing at him and jeering. His short legs began running, straight out of the school gate and back to his own home. He rushed upstairs and flung himself on the bed, sobbing.

When he woke up he found that the pillow was cold and damp. He remembered his dream, and scrambled to the mirror. 'Who am I?' he thought, half afraid that he would see Shortie Stewart's face staring back at him. But no, there he was, Robert Mackie, his hair all tousled, and his eyes heavy with sleep.

'Poor Stewart,' he kept thinking on the way to school. 'It must be awful for him not to have any friends, and not to be able to see properly.'

Stewart was standing by the wall of the playground, polishing his glasses.

'Come on, Stewart, you can join my gang — and we'll have a game of football at playtime,' he said, offering him a sweet.

'Hey, Robert,' shouted Big Bob across the playground. 'What are you doing with old Shortie Stewart? Come and play with us instead!'

Robert looked down at Stewart's feet. 'I just put myself in his shoes,' he said, and smiled.

Alternative story: Grace Halsell's transformation

Not very long ago, a woman named Grace Halsell walked though the streets of one of the biggest cities in America. In one particular district black people lived, crowded together in dirty, tumbledown houses. Grace noticed how badly these black people were treated by some of the white Americans. She asked why it was, and wondered what it must feel like to be treated in this way, but being white herself, she never seemed to find out. But Grace was determined to find out. Through friends who were willing to help her, she discovered there were certain pills she could take, and special sun-ray treatment she could have, that would turn her skin dark brown.

At the end of several months she was ready to put herself in the same position as one of the black women. She dressed in the same sort of clothes as they wore, and started on her voyage of discovery. First, she had to find herself a room in one of the large overcrowded tenement blocks, and then she set out to find a job so that she would have enough money to live on. Everywhere she went she found herself being treated with little respect and very little kindness. Jobs were unfairly given to white people, when she was as

17

well-qualified as they were, and when at last she managed to find one, she was expected to work very long hours for little pay. She discovered that white people did not always want to talk to her, or to sit next to her on the buses, and at certain clubs and cafés she was turned away because of her colour. Some churches refused to let her worship with the white congregation. She knew what it felt like to be black.

When Grace's dark colour faded she went away to live in another city, but she was determined to begin a long campaign to fight for the rights of her black friends all over America. There were many changes she wanted to see, but she knew those changes would not come quickly, or be easy to enforce. First, she had to change the attitudes and outlooks of the white people who were causing the people with dark skins to suffer.

For just a little while, Grace Halsell had put herself 'in someone else's shoes' and had felt and suffered as that person felt and suffered.

Prayer

We know people who are lonely and frightened, O God. We can see them every day in our school. Sometimes we are unkind to them. Help us to stand still for a moment and imagine what it would be like to be as they are, unloved, and often unlovely. Only when we begin to feel as they feel, and see as they see, will we be able to understand them and help them.

Readings

Jesus told of a time when he, as king, would sit upon his throne. He would summon the people to him and separate them as an Eastern shepherd separates his sheep from his goats. He would call the good people righteous, and say they were like the sheep, and the bad people were like the goats. He would call the righteous people to sit at his right hand to enjoy his kingdom. He would say to them:

'Come and possess the kingdom which has been prepared for you ever since the creation of the world. I was hungry and you fed me, thirsty and you gave me a drink; I was a stranger and you received me in your home, naked and you clothed me; I was sick and you took care of me, in prison and you visited me.'

The righteous will then answer him, 'When, Lord, did we ever see you hungry and feed you, or thirsty and give you drink? When did we ever see you a stranger and welcome you in our homes, or naked and clothe you? When did we ever see you sick or in prison, and visit you?' The King will reply, 'I tell you, whenever you did this for one of the least important of these brothers of mine, you did it for me!'

(Matthew 25.34-40, GNB)

A Jewish teacher once asked Jesus what was the most important commandment cr law.

Jesus answered, ' "Love the Lord your God with all your heart, with all your
soul, and with all your mind." This is the greatest and the most important
commandment. The second most important commandment is like it: "Love
your neighbour as you love yourself." '

(Matthew 22.37-39, GNB)

Hymns
Heavenly Father, may thy blessing
Kum ba yah
One man's hands   (SM 21)

Follow-up for the class-room

1   Have a selection of pictures of children in a variety of circumstances; use
Christian Aid posters, and pictures from newspapers, missionary and other
magazines, etc. Display the pictures and ask the class how they think the
children in the pictures feel. Encourage them to write two or three sentences
on how they would feel if they looked like the children in the pictures.

2   Each child in the class writes about a time when he or she felt nobody
understood them. On a narrow strip of paper, they should then write in bold

letters the main feeling they had at the time, eg, 'I
was afraid', 'I was lonely'. A large pair of shoes
should be drawn on a poster, or a real pair
attached to a display board, into which all the
strips of paper are put. Add the title 'Putting
myself in someone else's shoes'. Provide oppor-
tunity for the children to take out the slips and look at them; it will be helpful
for them to discover that other people have the same feelings of loneliness or
fear as they themselves have.

Put into writing

The Assembly

Preparation
Enlarge the illustration of a papyrus plant. Make a simple scroll to show: a piece of paper rolled from one end, and tied with a ribbon. Have a book ready to show.

Talk: Discoveries
(Hold up picture of papyrus) This is a picture of a plant which was very important to the people of Ancient Egypt. It grew very thickly on the banks of the River Nile, and was called 'papyrus'. The Egyptians soon discovered that it was not only beautiful, but very useful, too. They used the very soft part inside the stems as food, the feathery tops of the plant were woven to make sandals and baskets, and the roots made good fuel. But they used the stems themselves for the most important thing.

The stems were sliced into ribbons and hammered flat. Layers were gummed together and dried in the sun; then they were polished with a stone until they were smooth and hard. The sheets were then gummed together in a long line, and made into a book. Not a book as we know it today *(show one)*, but into a scroll book *(show scroll)*.

The book was written on by a scribe using a pen which had been made from a reed and sharpened with a pen-knife. The ink was soot mixed with gum and water. When finished, the book was rolled up like this *(demonstrate)* and tied with string (also made from papyrus), and then often sealed with wax. Sometimes the scrolls, or books, were stored in long, thin, pottery jars.

Many miles away to the north of Egypt, the people in the city of Byblos had learnt how to make this writing paper really well. They imported the papyrus reeds from Egypt, and then sold the paper far and wide. In Greece the word for book became *Biblos*. What does that remind you of? (Bible) And we get the word 'paper' from papyrus.

20

Many of the books in the Bible were first written on papyrus scrolls. Some were written on scrolls made of dried animal skin. Some scrolls were only discovered in 1947, when some of your parents were children. This is how it happened.

Right down near the Dead Sea, in Israel, where it is hot and dry and dusty, and there is little shelter from the scorching sun, tribes of wandering Bedouins take their sheep and goats up into the hills in search of food. One day two shepherd boys went to look for a straying animal. As they went they kicked at the stones, and then began picking them up to see how far they could throw them. 'Look, there's an opening in the cliff,' said one of them. 'Let's try to throw stones into it.' 'Perhaps it's a cave,' said the other, and they tossed their stones at the small opening.

Suddenly there was the sound of something breaking, as one of the stones went spinning through the hole in the rock-face. For a few moments they stood still, wondering what they had done. 'Let's go and see,' said one of the boys, and they scrambled up the dangerous cliff side. Squeezing themselves through the hole, they could see that it opened out into a cave. The pebble they had thrown was lying on the ground of the cave, surrounded by little bits of broken pottery. Almost buried by years of dust and sand lay more pottery: long, lidded jars — and they weren't empty. Most of them held rotting scrolls, the ink faint with age.

And that was the beginning of the discovery of the very earliest fragments of the scrolls from which some of the books of the Bible were copied. What excitement it caused! Newspapers were full of it, and the radio and newsreels gave it great coverage. How important those two boys must have felt!

Readings
In the Old Testament part of the Bible there is a story about the discovery of a scroll book. It was a book of God's laws and was found when the temple was being repaired. The young king, Josiah, heard about it, read it, and was shocked when he realised how the laws had been forgotten and neglected over the years. He wanted all his people to go back to following God as they should.

King Josiah summoned all the leaders of Judah and Jerusalem, and together they went to the Temple, accompanied by the priests and the prophets and all the rest of the people, rich and poor alike. Before them all, the king read aloud the whole book of the covenant which had been found in the Temple. He stood by the royal column and made a covenant with the Lord to obey him, to keep his laws and commands with all his heart and soul, and to put into practice the demands attached to the covenant, as written in the book. And all the people promised to keep the covenant.

(2 Kings 23.1-3, GNB)

21

Here is a reading from the book of Isaiah. One of the scrolls found by the shepherd boys was a very old 'edition' of the book of Isaiah.

In days to come
  the mountain where the Temple stands
  will be the highest one of all,
  towering above all the hills.
Many nations will come streaming to it,
  and their people will say,
'Let us go up the hill of our Lord,
  to the Temple of Israel's God.
He will teach us what he wants us to do;
  we will walk in the paths he has chosen.
For the Lord's teaching comes from Jerusalem;
  from Zion he speaks to his people.'
He will settle disputes among great nations.
They will hammer their swords into ploughs
  and their spears into pruning-knives.
Nations will never again go to war,
  never prepare for battle again.

(Isaiah 2.2-4, GNB)

Prayer
The response should be said or sung.
For being able to learn to read and write:
  We thank you, Lord God.
For paper and pens, for crayons and felt-tipped pens,
  We thank you, Lord God.
For books of stories, books of facts and figures, atlases, dictionaries and diaries:
  We thank you, Lord God.
For the Bible, which has been passed down to us through so many years:
  We thank you, Lord God.
That our lives are rich with knowledge because of those who write and report, illustrate and comment:
  We thank you, Lord God.

Hymns
The ink is black, the page is white   (CP 67, SM 10)
The Lord's my shepherd
The wise may bring their learning

22

Follow-up for the class-room

1   Learn about cuneiform writing from books. Make tablets of modelling clay, and write on them with wedge-shaped sticks.

2   Make a model papyrus scroll. Draw the papyrus plant. Make a list of, or collect samples of and label, the different kinds of paper that are used today.

3   Talk about pictograms, and follow this by looking at and discussing ideographs (road signs, mathematical signs, etc). Make charts of each.

4   Make a collection and display as many different versions of the Bible as can be found, and of Bible story books. Compare them.

Obstacles

The Assembly

Story: The obstacle race

Phil never expected to win the race. He didn't really like games at all — his legs never went as fast as everyone else's. He had once taken part in a cross-country run, but he'd been left far behind. He had just walked the last hundred yards because no one else was in sight. Mother said it was because he wasn't very tall, and Father said he couldn't expect to be strong if he didn't eat up all his cabbage.

But here Phil was, on the school sports day, waiting to be called for the obstacle race. He hadn't bothered to enter for the running races, or the jumping events, because he didn't want to come last and let his house down.

'You must all go in for somehting,' Miss Drage had said. His friend, Tony, didn't like running either, and had put his name down for the slow bicycle race, but Phil's bike needed a new wheel and couldn't be relied on to carry him, even very slowly, over the bumpy grass of the school playing field.

A whistle blew and Phil wished he could pretend he'd gone home with a bad cold. Perhaps he could just sit where he was behind Big Barry and no one would see him. But he knew that the boys at the starting line would be counted and he would be missed, and then he would have to stand up and climb over his friends, and everyone would stare at him. So he assembled with the others, forcing himself to smile and jump up and down, as if he was looking forward to the event. He looked at the line of boys standing with him. He was sure they were all bigger than him, and could run much faster.

Mr Farley was explaining the race. 'You must run first to the white flag,' he said.

Phil peered into the distance: even the white flag seemed to be much too far away.

'Then you will find a pole fixed across the course,' the teacher went on. 'You can jump it, or scramble over it. After that you'll find we've filled the dip with water which you have to go through.'

Phil was beginning to wish he'd gone in for the egg and spoon race.

'Run to the hoops,' went on Mr Farley, 'and get through the two that are in front of you; then you must crawl under the net and out at the other end. After

24

that you must slide through the drain pipe tubes and run to the finishing rope.' He looked along the line of boys to make sure they had understood. 'On your marks; get set; go!'

Phil ran as hard as he could. The white flag seemed to be a mile away. At last he reached it, but the other boys were already over the pole by the time he arrived. He threw himself at the pole and landed with a thump in the sand on the other side. The water dip was churned with mud, but he slid into it quickly and gasped at the coldness of the water. It wasn't very deep, though, and his shoes held well on the slippery ground. Two boys were floundering beside him, unable to get a grip to scramble up the bank on the other side. Phil ran to the hoops: they were rather small, but he had no difficulty twisting through them. He noticed that Tubby Brooks had got stuck in one of his! Phil was glad he was thin and small.

He reached the net spread on the grass like a giant trap. It hadn't looked so big from a distance. Two boys were already struggling through it, and one of them looked hopelessly entangled. Making sure that he would head off in a straight line, Phil knelt and squirmed under the net, the grass damp and soft under his body. He daren't lift his head to see if he was going in the right direction, and he kept his arms and elbows as close to his body as he could. He felt the net lifting behind him, and heard a boy panting hard as he crept closer. The boy's hand touched Phil's shoe and pulled at it. He was trying to slow Phil down! Phil was going to give a good kick, but at that moment his foot shot out of his training shoe and he was free. Like a grass snake he slithered away under the net and suddenly found himself free of it.

Phil stood up, panting hard, and was thankful to see that the drain pipe tubes were straight ahead of him. No one else was sliding through them. Phil hoped they hadn't all left him behind. 'But I'm not last, anyway,' he said to himself, thinking of the boy who had so unfairly grabbed his shoe under the net. He rushed for the tubes, feeling the ground uneven and stony under his bare foot. Again, he was glad he was rather small and thin, because getting through the tubes was easy. He made himself into a long snake-shape and pulled himself along until his head emerged into the sunshine.

'Now I've got to run!' he said aloud. He heard boys cheering.

'Come on, Phil!' they shouted from the finishing line. Phil ran as if he was electrically charged, his legs rushing over the grass as if they didn't belong to him. He didn't even notice how uncomfortable it was with only one shoe. He touched the rope and a great cheer went up. Someone slapped him on the back.

'Well done, young Philip,' said Mr Farley. 'The house needed someone like you to win points — you were small enough to do it — and you didn't give up!'

Phil was worn out, and breathless, as he turned and looked back at the obstacles. It certainly hadn't been easy, but he'd won the race!

You will find, as you grow older, that the whole of life is rather like an obstacle race: there will be plenty of things to stop you going right on! Remember, in any obstacle race you need plenty of patience, and a great deal of determination, to get to the finishing post.

Readings

The person who wrote one of the letters to the first Jewish-Christians was probably thinking of a race like this when he wrote:

As for us, we have this large crowd of witnesses round us. So then, let us rid ourselves of everything that gets in the way, and of the sin which holds on to us so tightly, and let us run with determination the race that lies before us. Let us keep our eyes fixed on Jesus, on whom our faith depends from beginning to end. Think of what he went through; how he put up with so much hatred from sinners! So do not let yourselves become discouraged and give up.

(Hebrews 12.1-2a,3, GNB)

Jesus warned his friends that it would not be easy to keep on following him. He said:

'Be on your guard. You will be handed over to the courts. You will be flogged in synagogues. You will be summoned to appear before governors and kings on my account to testify in their presence. But before the end the Gospel must be proclaimed to all nations. So when you are arrested and taken away, do not worry about what you will say. All will hate you for your allegiance to me; but the man who holds out to the end will be saved.'

(Mark 13.9-11a,13, NEB)

Prayer

The response after each part of the prayer is: Help us to carry on, O Lord.

When we find we have difficult work to do,
    Help us to carry on, O Lord.
When people seem unfriendly and unfair to us,
    Help us to carry on, O Lord.
When we are ill, tired, or discouraged,
    Help us to carry on, O Lord.
When we are cross or miserable, and have to try really hard to be pleasant to others,
    Help us to carry on, O Lord.

26

When we wonder if we will ever be able to love and serve you as we should,
   Help us to carry on, O Lord.
Help us to overcome the obstacles that hold us back, and to keep on going
with determination, O Lord.

Hymns
He who would valiant be
Soldiers of Christ, arise
The journey of life   (CP 45)

Follow-up for the class-room

1   Let each child work out on paper a plan for an obstacle race. The best, or
the most interesting, might be tried out during a games or PE lesson.

2   Copy a fairly difficult problem or crossword puzzle on to the board, and
let the children see who can actually finish it; do not make it a race, simply a
'battle of endurance'. Less able children could try colouring a large and
complicated design, or making one of their own on paper marked out in
small squares.

3   Introduce and explain the word 'perseverance'. Talk about times when
this is needed, and let the children add their contributions. Encourage them
to draw or write about a time when they met obstacles and needed
perseverance to keep going.

Additional story: Nehemiah's perseverance
Nehemiah lived in Persia, many years before Jesus was born. He worked in a
king's palace in an honoured position, but he worked there because he was a
prisoner, not because he had chosen to do so. Often he longed to be free so
that he could go back to Jerusalem where his family had lived for years.
   One day some travellers from Judah came to the king's palace. They
brought bad news to Nehemiah: the Jews who had been left in Jerusalem
after the Persian invasion were in great difficulties, and were very unhappy.
The beautiful wall around Jerusalem was still in ruins, and the gates,
destroyed by fire, had never been replaced. Foreigners who lived just outside
Jerusalem were threatening to attack.
   Nehemiah felt sorry for the Jews in Jerusalem, and determined that

somehow he would return there and help them. But he was a prisoner, so the first obstacle he had to overcome was the one of getting away. Escape was impossible, but even if it had been simple it would have been out of the question to travel alone, and on foot, the long distance back to Jerusalem. Nehemiah prayed, 'Help me, O God.'

The king noticed Nehemiah's unhappy face. 'What is it?' he asked. 'You are not ill, so something terrible must have happened to make you look like this.'

Nehemiah told the king everything, and begged to be allowed to leave Persia long enough to return to Jerusalem and help his people rebuild their beloved city. The king was sympathetic, and let him go; he even sent soldiers and horses to accompany Nehemiah on his journey.

Even before he reached Jerusalem, Nehemiah realised that he would have to face serious problems. The neighbouring foreigners did not want anyone to attempt the rebuilding of Jerusalem. For three days after his arrival Nehemiah did nothing. Then, in the middle of the night, he set out on a donkey to inspect the ruins of the walls. The broken bricks and rubble still lay about, making it difficult for them to make their way.

Later that day Nehemiah called the Jewish people together and told them his plans. He told them that together, with determination and God's help, they could do the work. So they began to rebuild.

It took only a short time for the unfriendly neighbours to realise what was happening. They stood around laughing. 'What do you think you're doing?' they asked.

'We trust God,' replied Nehemiah, 'and he will help us.'

Their enemies came back again and again. 'What are these miserable Jews doing?' they jeered. 'Are they thinking of rebuilding the whole city? Can they make stones out of this rubble?'

'What kind of a wall can they build?' scorned another. 'It won't be strong enough to keep out a fox!'

But Nehemiah carried on. The Jews, too, felt his courage and determination, and soon the walls were half built. Their enemies realised that the Jews were not put off by mockery, and they became angry. They began to make plans for more serious assault. But Nehemiah was ready; when he heard from his spies of their plans, he put his own into action.

'Don't be afraid of them,' he told his people. 'We'll be ready for them, because we believe that God wants us to restore our city, and will help us.'

From then on half the men worked on the walls while half stood guard, and even the men carrying the building materials were armed against sudden attack. The builders themselves had swords by their sides, and a trumpeter was stationed in such a position that every man could hear his warning notes in case of sudden danger.

'If you hear the trumpet,' said Nehemiah, 'come to me at once, and we'll fight to keep our walls safe.'

28

And so the work went on every day, and at night the walls were still guarded carefully. Nehemiah himself never gave up vigil. Even at night he slept with his clothes on, and with his sword by his side.

In two months the work on the wall was complete. The neighbouring foreigners had tried their hardest to stop the rebuilding, but had not been able to fight against Nehemiah's firm determination and perseverance, and his absolute certainty of God's support.

(From Nehemiah 1—2;4;6.15-16)

Who is my neighbour?

The Assembly

It is suggested that the Bible reading should come first in this Assembly, as either of the two stories would be more meaningful if told after it.

Reading
We usually think of neighbours as those people who live close to us, next door, or in the same street. But Jesus put a wider meaning on the word:

A teacher of the Law came up and tried to trap Jesus. 'Teacher,' he asked, 'what must I do to receive eternal life?'

Jesus answered him, 'What do the Scriptures say? How do you interpret them?'

The man answered, ' "Love the Lord your God with all your heart, with all your soul, with all your strength, and with all your mind"; and "Love your neighbour as you love yourself." '

'You are right,' Jesus replied; 'do this and you will live.'

But the teacher of the Law wanted to justify himself, so he asked Jesus, 'Who is my neighbour?'

Jesus answered, 'There was once a man who was going down from Jerusalem to Jericho when robbers attacked him, stripped him, and beat him up, leaving him half dead. It so happened that a priest was going down that road; but when he saw the man, he walked on by, on the other side. In the same way a Levite also came along, went over and looked at the man, and then walked on by, on the other side. But a Samaritan who was travelling that way came upon the man, and when he saw him, his heart was filled with pity. He went over to him, poured oil and wine on his wounds and bandaged them; then he put the man on his own animal and took him to an inn, where he took care of him. The next day he took out two silver coins and gave them to the innkeeper. "Take care of him," he told the innkeeper, "and when I come back this way, I will pay you whatever else you spend on him." '

And Jesus concluded, 'In your opinion, which one of these three acted like a neighbour towards the man attacked by the robbers?'

The teacher of the Law answered, 'The one who was kind to him.'
Jesus replied, 'You go, then, and do the same.'

(Luke 10.25-37, GNB)

Story: My neighbour
Roy and his friends at school laughed at John because he wore glasses and
wasn't any good at games. One day John thought they were being friendly
when they said, 'Come and try this "assault course" with us.'

They had fixed up chairs, tables and ropes across the room, and the idea
was to cross from one side to the other without touching the floor. The others
did it first, and then it was John's turn.

'Let's take one of the chairs away,' whispered Roy. 'John's so short-
sighted he won't notice!'

So, when John swung himself across to the chair, he fell with a thud. The
others laughed, but John began to moan.

'He's hurt!' said Roy. They went to fetch a grown-up, and the grown-up
sent for an ambulance. John had broken his wrist and was taken to hospital.

That night Roy told his mother what had happened. 'That was an unkind
thing to do,' she said. 'You must think of something to make John feel better.'

Next day Roy went to see John. He looked pale, and his wrist was in plaster.
'I'm sorry,' said Roy. 'We didn't think ...'

'Don't worry,' said John. 'I think you're a "good Samaritan" to come and
see me like this.'

'The good Samaritan took the wounded man to an inn and made him
comfortable,' said Roy. 'I didn't do that for you!'

'But you've done something good for me,' said John. 'What I needed most
was a friend, and I think I've got one now.'

Alternative story: Help!
Julie always left school the minute she could. It wasn't that she wanted to get
away from the building, or from the other girls, it was simply so that she could
be one of the first to arrive at the bus-stop. There was always such a crowd:
girls from her own school, smaller children from the school down the road,
and dozens of girls who poured out of St Grants school opposite. She disliked
them: they had posh blue uniforms and loud voices and hockey sticks.
Sometimes she had to sit next to one of them on the bus, and she always tried
not to let herself be touched by them, by making herself as small as possible.

Today she was sure the school clock had been wrong. The bell was always
rung at 4 o'clock sharp, but today it went when her watch said five to four. She
had been the first person out of the school gate. If she was very lucky, she might
be able to get the earlier bus, and be well away before the St Grants girls came.

31

No one was at the bus-stop except two older boys. She stood there panting, then decided to look in her purse to make sure she had her bus fare. As she opened the purse, she heard the bus turn the corner. And then things happened so quickly that she couldn't be quite sure about them afterwards. The purse was knocked from her hand by one of the boys standing there, the other leant down and grabbed it, the bus stopped, the boys leapt on, and the conductor rang the bell. Julie was left with her mouth open and her head spinning. She ran a little way after the bus, waving her hand and calling, but no one heard, and she walked slowly back to the bus-stop. She had to sit down on the bench to think.

'Hi, Julie,' said her friend, Carol, walking up. 'Got your homework? You look a bit worried.'

'Yes, I ...' Julie began, but Carol had already turned away, looking for the bus. Two more of Julie's school friends walked by, smiling at her as they passed. Julie wanted to tell them what had happened but, as she opened her mouth to speak, they ran on, racing each other home. More people gathered at the stop, and the girls from St Grants were crossing the road, in a straggling, menacing mass. The next bus was just turning the corner.

'Carol, wait,' called Julie, but Carol was already climbing the stairs of the bus, followed by posh blue uniforms and hockey sticks. Julie didn't dare to get on. She had no money for the bus fare, and everyone would laugh and point at her when she told the bus-conductor. She knew he would let her ride on the bus if she gave him her name and address, but she would NOT be laughed at by those girls of St Grants!

She went back to the bench to sit and wait for the next bus. Just at that moment some more girls in blue crossed the road, joking and jostling as they reached the bus-stop. Julie felt very miserable, and very small, and she began to cry quietly. How would she ever get home?

'Here, what's up?' said a voice near her. A St Grants girl was sitting beside her on the bench. 'What's the matter?' she asked again.

Julie's first thought was to edge away, as the blue uniform got near her ordinary black blazer. Instead, she found herself telling the girl what had happened. 'So I've got no money — I'll never get home!' she wailed.

'Here,' said the stranger. 'I've got some spare money. I was going to get some sweets, but you'd better have it for your fare. You can give it back to me tomorrow, if you like.'

Julie looked up. The St Grants girl looked friendly. 'Thanks very much,' Julie said, and took the money. A bus swung round the corner.

'This your bus?' asked the girl. 'I'm going on it, too. Let's sit together.'

Julie was so glad of her protection as the blue uniforms pushed and grabbed at the empty seats. The kind girl was already standing by one of the seats, guarding it. 'I'm saving this for my friend,' she said, as someone tried to sit on it.

Julie edged towards her. 'Am I your friend?' she asked.

'Of course,' the girl replied.

Julie moved along the seat, feeling the blue uniform warm against her hand. 'Thanks a lot,' she whispered.

Alternative or additional reading

Jesus was always quick to help his 'neighbours', especially those who were ill, or lonely, or very poor. Here is a story about him healing someone who was handicapped and a beggar:

They came to Jericho, and as Jesus was leaving with his disciples and a large crowd, a blind beggar named Bartimaeus son of Timaeus was sitting by the road. When he heard that it was Jesus of Nazareth, he began to shout, 'Jesus! Son of David! Take pity on me!'

Many of the people scolded him and told him to be quiet. But he shouted even more loudly, 'Son of David, take pity on me!'

Jesus stopped and said, 'Call him.'

So they called the blind man. 'Cheer up!' they said. 'Get up, he is calling you.'

He threw off his cloak, jumped up, and came to Jesus.

'What do you want me to do for you?' Jesus asked him.

'Teacher,' the blind man answered, 'I want to see again.'

'Go,' Jesus told him, 'your faith has made you well.'

At once he was able to see and followed Jesus on the road.

(Mark 10.46-52, GNB)

Prayer

Help us, O God, to recognise need in other people, and to give help whenever we can, even to those whom we do not like. May we remember that all people are our neighbours, whether they are friends or enemies, and that Jesus asks us, and expects us, to help them.

Hymns

Jesus, Lord, we look to thee
When I needed a neighbour
Would you walk by on the other side   (CP 70)

Music

Song: Streets of London.

Follow-up for the class-room

1   Talk about the story of the good Samaritan. Write the following list on the board and ask the children to copy it, numbering, in order of importance, the things about the Samaritan:
He carried ointment and bandages.
He had a donkey with him.
He was concerned about someone who needed help.
He gave his time.
He had money to give to the innkeeper.

2   Plan a project of help for a person, or a group of people, in need, eg, a sick pupil, old people, victims of earthquake or other disaster, a local charity, etc.

3   Ask the children to imagine living alone on a desert island. When would they miss other people's help and company most? Discuss this or write about it.

4   Dramatise or illustrate the story of the good Samaritan.

Advent adventure

The Assembly

Preparation

Very little preparation is needed for this Assembly, but you might like to have ready placards bearing the words used, ie, ADVENT — TOWARDS THE COMING, and ADVENTURE — ABOUT TO HAPPEN.

Talk

Everyone has started to think about Christmas. How can we tell that the festival is coming? *(Get suggestions and answers)* The calendar tells us; we've begun to practise Christmas carols; we're planning to make presents; the shops are decorated, and some of the streets *(Refer to local preparations)*. What about at home? Has mother made a Christmas cake yet, or a pudding? Have you been telling people what presents you want? Have you heard about plans for visitors, or about visits that your family are going to make?

Many people have been busy planning Christmas for months and months: new designs for Christmas cards were chosen as long ago as last January, and were printed in June or July. Catalogues of Christmas toys were prepared in the summer, and shops ordered their Christmas stocks of clothes, games and food a long time ago. Record companies made Christmas discs in August, and even here, in school, we had meetings near the beginning of this term to decide what our Christmas celebrations would be this year.

Perhaps you've heard the word ADVENT. We are near the Church's Advent Sunday. The word means TOWARDS THE COMING. It comes from two Latin words, AD, meaning towards, and VENIRE, the coming. Can you think of another word that begins with advent and that means doing something rather daring or exciting? (ADVENTURE) In the old Roman form this meant ABOUT TO HAPPEN, which is almost the same. So, at ADVENT we are looking forward to a coming which is an ADVENTURE: it is ABOUT TO HAPPEN. Christmas for us is about to happen; we've only two or three weeks to wait. We are waiting for the holidays, presents, parties, pantomimes and special food. But remember we are waiting, too, to celebrate the coming of a baby, a baby who grew to be a man, a man who changed the whole world.

35

Thousands and thousands of years ago, when Moses taught the Israelite people God's laws, they believed that they were God's chosen people, and that he would lead and protect them. Hundreds of years later they still believed this, and when things were going right for them, when they were happy and peaceful, they could not think that there might be difficult times ahead. But trouble came, the kingdom was divided, and there were terrible wars. Still the Israelite people said, 'God has chosen us; he will provide for us and protect us.' Then, in the middle of their dangers and difficulties, a preacher told them some good news. 'God will send a ruler for Israel,' he said, 'and his people will live in safety. He will bring peace.'

The Israelite people waited; they believed the preacher. In their very darkest days they clung to this promise: 'A king will come to deliver you.' But they had to wait a very long time, not just two or three weeks, or even months, but years and years and years. Old men would tell their children, and their grandchildren, about the promise, and all the people of Israel held the secret hope in their hearts that one day, one day, they would have to suffer no more.

Like all the other people, a girl called Mary looked forward to the day when the Messiah, the promised one, would come. By now the people were suffering even more: their country had been over-run and occupied by forces from the great Roman Empire, and they were desperately unhappy. Mary never dreamt, or even hoped, that she would be the first to know about the Messiah's coming, and it was beyond her wildest dreams that he would come to her!

One day she was visited by an angel, a special messenger from God. The angel said:

'Peace be with you! The Lord is with you and has greatly blessed you.'

Mary was deeply troubled and wondered what his words meant. The angel said to her, 'Don't be afraid, Mary; God has been gracious to you. You will give birth to a son, and you will name him Jesus. He will be great and will be called the Son of the Most High God. The Lord God will make him a king, and his kingdom will never end!' *(Part of Luke 1.28-33,GNB)*

So Mary had a wonderful secret. The Messiah was coming at last; the waiting time would soon be over.

Reading
The preacher Micah told the Israelite people about the coming of a king who would save his people:

The Lord says, 'Bethlehem Ephrathah, you are one of the smallest towns in Judah, but out of you I will bring a ruler for Israel, whose family line goes back to ancient times.'

When he comes he will rule his people with the strength that comes from the Lord and with the majesty of the Lord God himself. His people will live in safety because people all over the earth will acknowledge his greatness, and he will bring peace.

(Micah 2.2,4-5a, GNB)

Hymns
Go, tell it on the mountain   (CP 24, SM 14)
It came upon the midnight clear
Unto us a boy is born

Prayer
Help us to remember, Lord Jesus, that it is only because you came as a baby on that first Christmas day that we can look forward to this Christmas with such excitement. Thank you for all that you have done for the world.

Music
Britten: A ceremony of carols.

Follow-up for the class-room

1 Read together the story of the Annunciation, in Luke 1.26-38.

2 Write a new carol or poem, telling of looking forward to Christmas.

3 Look up the words of the carol 'Unto us a boy is born' and compare them with the words of Isaiah 9.6.

4 Make a list of the signs telling that Christmas is coming. Make plans for a class project on giving.

5 Make a Christmas frieze for the class-room.

Considering the heavens

The Assembly

Preparation

You will need a large sheet of blue paper, firmly fixed to a blackboard or wall; a semi-circular piece of black paper; a narrow strip of grey paper, as wide as the bottom of the semi-circle, and cut at the top to represent the earth-line; a sun, moon, and four pillars; chalk.

Talk

Thousands of years ago, the Hebrew people believed the stars were lights, hung in the sky by God. They also thought that God fixed in the sky two brighter lights: the sun to give us daylight *(fix sun to the diagram)*; and the moon to provide a more gentle light when people were sleeping *(fix moon to diagram)*. We know now that some stars are suns with planets like our own. They also thought that the sky was semi-circular *(as this one is)*, and had a covering like a huge domed ceiling. *(Draw this in with a chalk line)* This was called the firmament.

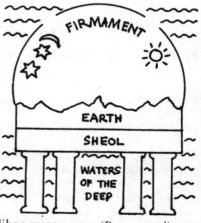

High above this ceiling there was water like a great ocean. *(Draw wavy lines to indicate this)* In the firmament, or ceiling, they believed that God had made holes through which the water above could fall as rain on the earth. *(Rub holes in the chalk ceiling)* The earth, they thought, was completely flat, and underneath it was another land, called Sheol, which was inhabited by spirits of the dead people who had once lived on the land. The whole of the earth and Sheol was supported on huge pillars *(fix on)* and was lifted above the Waters of the Deep, which were all around.

In Greece, even in very early times, there were men — astronomers — who studied the stars. They, too, thought that the world was flat, and that it floated about on the water. A man called Ptolemy thought that the earth was still and that it was the sun, moon and stars which moved around it in patterns. It was not until about 1610 that a man first looked at the heavens through a telescope. His name was Galileo.

Nowadays enormous telescopes have been built, and in recent years men have discovered how to send exploration machines into space so that they can study the stars and the planets at closer range.

Our earth seems big; but it isn't until we look up at the millions of other worlds shining in the night sky that we realise how huge the universe is, and how very small we are.

Readings

The account of God's creation of the universe was told from father to son through many generations until it was written down. Here is a modern translation:

'Let there be a vault,' said God,
   'separating the waters above the vault
     from the waters on the earth below!'
The great vault was made;
   he called it 'sky'.

'Let there be lights in the sky,' said God,
   'marking off day from night,
signs for festivals,
   for seasons and years!
Let the lights of the sky
   shine down on the earth!'
He made the sun,
   dominating the day,
the moon and the stars
   dominating the night —
he set them in the sky
   to shine on the earth,
     day and night,
     light and darkness —
       splendid in his eyes.

(Part of Genesis 1.6-8,14-18, WQ)

The psalms of the Bible were often chanted as songs by the people of Israel. In this way they praised God for his great creation.

Whither shall I go from thy Spirit?
  Or whither shall I flee from thy presence?
If I ascend to heaven, thou art there!
  If I make my bed in Sheol, thou art there!
If I take the wings of the morning
  and dwell in the uttermost parts of the sea,
even there thy hand shall lead me,
  and thy right hand shall hold me.
If I say, 'Let only darkness cover me,
  and the light about me be night,'
even the darkness is not dark to thee,
  the night is bright as the day;
  for darkness is as light with thee.

(Psalm 139.7-12, RSV)

From very earliest days, men and women have looked up at the sky and marvelled at the wonder of God's heaven. One of the writers of the psalms made up this poem for the people to sing:

When I look at the sky, which you have made,
  at the moon and the stars, which you set in their places —
what is man, that you think of him;
  mere man, that you care for him?

(Psalm 8.3-4, GNB)

Prayer
Great God, maker of the world we know, and of all the worlds that we see at night, hear our prayer. You are so great and wonderful that we feel we have no words to speak, no songs or hymns that can adequately show our praise, and no intelligence that can fully grasp the enormity of your creation. But we do know that Jesus came into the world to tell us that each of us is important to you, and that you have a special love for every one of us here. Thank you, great God, that we can come to you as a loving Father.

Hymns
Can you count the stars that brightly
Praise the Lord, ye heavens adore him
Who can count the stars   (SM 56)

Poem
Dots of glistening brightness
large and small;
patterns, each one beautiful,
ordered and particular,
are in the sky for all.
Some people glance above
when out at night:
'Will it rain?' they ask, 'or
does the clear sky mean frost?'
Some never even look,
keeping their eyes upon the road ahead,
thoughts full of what will happen on the earth:
when and where, how and why.
There, so beautiful above their heads,
so plain, so clear,
the evidence of God;
he is; from time began
to some far future. The stars
spell out his presence,
his security,
for those who lift their eyes to look.

Music
Sibelius: At the Castle Gate, from Pelléas and Mélisande Suite (The Sky at Night theme).
Holst: The Planets.

Follow-up for the class-room

1 Learn something about the Milky Way; the Earth is part of that galaxy. Why is it so called? What is it made up of? Discover the meaning of a galaxy. Consider the enormity of the Milky Way: a rocket travelling at 100,000 miles an hour would take 670,000,000 years to travel from one end to the other.

2 Make a large wall picture of the night sky; include the star groups that can be seen easily at night.

3 Make a model or collage of the Hebrew universe.

4   Collect pictures of star and planet explorations, radio telescopes, observatories etc; also facts, figures and reports from newspapers and magazines. Make these into a wall chart or scrapbook.

5   If it is near Christmas, connect the Assembly with the star in the East (Matthew 2.1-12). Discover the difference between astronomy and astrology, and collect examples of each.

6   Write out and decorate Psalm 8.3-4.

New Year and Epiphany

The Assembly

Story

This is a story about a man who made a long journey in the days before travel was simple and neighbouring countries were friendly. The man lived in Rome, in Italy, over thirteen hundred years ago, and had been chosen by the Pope to make a journey overland as far as a stretch of water, which he must somehow cross, and, beyond that channel of sea, to a small island. The Pope knew that on that island most of the people still worshipped their own heathen gods.

'Go there,' the Pope told the monk, Augustine, 'and tell them the good news of Jesus Christ.'

Augustine started well, full of plans and hopes for these wild people. He struggled on foot through the snow-capped mountains of the Alps and on into France, which in those days was called Gaul. There, as he travelled westwards, the people he met became fiercer and wilder. When he got near the coast he heard terrible stories about the people, called the Angles, who lived beyond the channel.

'The sea is a difficult one to cross,' he was warned, 'and, even if you escape death in a small boat, you're sure to be killed once you reach land the other side. The people there are just like wild beasts!'

Augustine was afraid. The journey was becoming far more difficult than anything he had imagined, and he didn't want to go on.

'The Pope must send someone else,' he told his companions. 'I'm just not well enough equipped to face these fierce people.'

And so, back across Gaul, through the Alps, and into his own country, he journeyed.

'I couldn't go on,' he told the Pope in Rome. 'Release me from my task. Send someone else to take the good news to the Angles.'

The Pope was disappointed, but still thought that Augustine should be the man to go. 'Once you've started something,' he said to the monk, 'you should continue it. Don't give up now.'

'Then I shall need more help,' said Augustine, expecting representatives of the Roman army to be sent with him.

'Your help will come from God,' replied the Pope. 'Go on, and trust in him. He is all you need.'

So, for the second time, Augustine set off with his small band of companions. This time, he spent a great deal of time in prayer, asking for strength and courage. At last they reached the coast of Gaul and set sail, across what is now the English Channel. They saw the white cliffs beyond, and sailed along the coast searching for a safe place to land. Soon they found a wide river estuary and sailed up it until they came to a small island — the Isle of Thanet — where they made their camp.

The journey from Rome was over; but for Augustine another great journey had just begun, because he looked at the work ahead of him and saw that he still had far to go. He spent over twenty years with the savage Angles, the people who would later be called the English. By the time of his death he had spread the good news of Jesus Christ far and wide, and Christianity had taken root in England.

Augustine journeyed — and every boy and girl here is about to do the same thing: begin a journey. Your journey will be a long one, lasting all the year. Yes, you've got a new year before you, months and months of travelling, and sometimes you will find it difficult to go on. Sometimes you, like Augustine, will feel like going back, giving up, refusing to look ahead and face what has to be done. Just try to remember that, like Augustine, you will need help, and you can get that help as he did, by trusting in God and asking for his strength and courage.

Lots of people make New Year Resolutions as they get ready for the journey through the year. You really only need one — to ask God to be with you.

Alternative talk

Preparation

Collect together as many of the following items as possible, and put most of them in a rucksack or case: goggles, thermos flask, large story book, map, sunglasses, bag of marbles and/or toy cars, model aeroplane, roller skates or football boots or flippers, tin of baked beans, pot plant or flowers, roll of paper, pack of cards, game such as ludo, small box marked first-aid, overcoat, wellington boots and a large cuddly toy. Have a blackboard and chalk ready to write: tin-opener, more food, hairbrush and comb, washing gear, change of clothes, torch. Rehearse responses with the child (boy or girl) taking part.

Talk

(Child comes on to platform loaded with rucksack or case, and carrying some items in arms as well)

Leader: Hello, where are you off to?

Child: I'm going camping.

Leader: Who with?

Child: Oh, by myself. It's a sort of test for my youth club.

Leader: Are you walking?

Child: Yes; all the way. We have to. But I don't think I'll make it.

Leader: You do look a bit loaded. Whatever are you taking with you?

Child: Oh, just a few things that might be useful.

Leader: A few things? Come on, let's have a look. *(Take articles one by one from the child, commenting on each as they are placed where everyone can see them)* I don't think all this is very sensible. Where's your tent?

Child: I don't need to take one. There's one on the camp-site already. There's a stove there, too.

Leader: What about food?

Child: I've got a tin of baked beans!

Leader: Have you got a tin-opener? *(Child looks a little foolish and shakes his head)* No. Well, we'll write that down. *(Write on blackboard)* I'm glad you've got a warm coat with you, you'll need that. Let's put all the things you *really* need on one side. *(Put baked beans and coat on one side)* What else has he got that would be useful? *(Invite suggestions from the school; you should end up with coat, baked beans, map, first-aid box, wellington boots and possibly one toy or game)* Now, has he got *everything* he will need? *(Invite suggestions again; you should include in this list such things as: more food, hairbrush and comb, washing gear, change of clothes, torch etc)* Right, we'll send you home for all those really essential things first. Before starting out again, leave all the things you don't need, at home.

That boy (or girl) was getting ready for a journey. Everybody here is about to do the same thing. It's a long journey, that will last until 31st December. You have a new year before you — months and months of journeying, and sometimes it will seem a very difficult journey. To make it easier, just make sure you take with you only the things you will really need, like kindness, honesty and thoughtfulness. And perhaps you can manage to carry a sense of humour with you, as a sort of extra. You can well do without loading yourselves up with things that will keep pulling you back, like laziness, or selfishness, or bullying.

Lots of people make New Year Resolutions as they pack their luggage for the journey through the year; you could make your resolution to be to carry only good things with you as you go.

Readings

Jesus once sent his disciples off on a journey, and he gave them instructions about what they would need on their journey. He said:

'Don't take anything with you on your journey except a stick — no bread, no beggar's bag, no money in your pockets. Wear sandals, but don't carry an extra shirt.'

(Mark 6.8-9, GNB)

They were to travel light, carrying nothing that would hamper them.

As Paul looked back over his life he saw it as a journey. Listen to what he said about it, and decide for yourselves whether it had been an easy one or not:

In my many travels I have been in danger from floods and from robbers, in danger from fellow-Jews and from Gentiles; there have been dangers in the cities, dangers in the wilds, dangers on the high seas, and dangers from false friends. There has been work and toil; often I have gone without sleep; I have been hungry and thirsty; I have often been without enough food, shelter or clothing.

(2 Corinthians 11.26-27, GNB)

Hymns

Lord of all hopefulness, Lord of all joy
Through the night of doubt and sorrow
The journey of life   (CP 45)

Prayer

Be with us, Lord God, at the beginning of our journey through the year. Help us as we decide on the things we must take with us, and give us the courage we shall need to leave behind all the things that will make the journey more difficult. You know what is best for each of us; may we put ourselves in your hands, today, and every day from now on.

Follow-up for the class-room

1   Discussion about New Year Resolutions. Some children may have made (and broken) them. Others could be encouraged to make them.

2   Tell the story of Gladys Aylward, the missionary who took a crowd of homeless Chinese children on a long and dangerous journey to safety. (A good library will provide reference for this.)

3   Instead of looking back to Christmas, with regret that it is over, encourage the children to look forward. Make a class list of all the things they can expect to enjoy during the year: Easter eggs, summer holidays, etc.

4   Make a clay model of the Roman god Janus, who had two faces: he looked back at the old year, and forward to the new — hence our name for the month of January.

5   Prepare an assembly for Epiphany (January 6) and present it to the school. Seven children and a leader should rehearse the dramatic presentation; other children should rehearse the poem, and prepare the prayer and reading.

Dramatic presentation Three children should be dressed as the wise men and should carry suitable gifts; three should wear no special clothing but should carry (a) school text and exercise books, (b) football boots and ball, or hockey stick and ball (as appropriate to the school), and (c) toys, collections and games. The seventh child should carry nothing. The children come from the back of the hall at appropriate times.

Leader: Jesus was born in the town of Bethlehem in Judaea, during the time when Herod was king. Soon afterwards, some men who studied the stars came from the east to Jerusalem and asked, 'Where is the baby born to be the king of the Jews?' *(Matthew 2.1-2a, GNB) (While this is being read the three wise men come slowly from the back of the hall. Quiet background music could be played as they come)* These men come from the east — far beyond the River Jordan. Are you kings?
First wise man: We are ordinary men — perhaps more learned than most. The Bible does not say we are kings.
Leader: Three wise men ...
Second wise man: There may have been more. The Bible does not tell us how many journeyed to find the king.
Leader: Why did you make the journey?
Third wise man: We are astrologers: we study the stars. We saw an unusually bright star, and from our charts we read that it would lead us to a child who would become the king of the Jews.
First wise man: The star seemed to lead us to Judaea. We came to find the king.
Leader: But you are not Jews, are you? Why look for the king of the Jews?
Second wise man: Any new king is important, and we think that this one will be

47

more important than most. We bring him gifts.

First wise man (holding his gift high): We bring gold ...

Second wise man (holding up his gift): ... and frankincense ...

Third wise man (holding up his gift): ... and myrrh. *(They lay down their gifts, and step to one side. The next three children come from the back)*

First child: We want to visit him, too. I bring him my work. *(Holds it high)*

Second child: I bring him my sport. *(Shows it)*

Third child: I bring him my play and my hobbies. *(Shows it. All three lay down their gifts)*

Leader: There's someone else coming. *(Seventh child hurries to the front)* What have you got to offer him? *(Child shrugs shoulders)* Have you brought him your work?

Child: No, it's not very good.

Leader: He could help you to do better. Have you brought him your sport?

Child: I don't like sport.

Leader: He could help you to enjoy it. Have you brought your play?

Child: I haven't got many toys. And I don't belong to any clubs, and I don't collect anything.

Leader: Then why have you come?

Child (shrugs shoulders again): I just love him, that's all.

Leader: Well, you have brought him something — the best thing of all — yourself and your love. What could be better? *(Pause; children return to their places)* January 6 is a special day in the Christian calendar, called Epiphany. This word is made up from two Greek words which mean 'to show forth' and it reminds us that Jesus was shown to the wise men. Traditionally there were three wise men who brought their gifts and gave them to Jesus, the gift which God had given to the world. The wise men gave, and we can give, because God has given to us — Jesus his Son. Coming at the start of a new year, this season of Epiphany can be a reminder to us that we can give and go on giving throughout the year. What will you give?

Hymn   Wise men seeking Jesus

Reading   Jesus said that it was no good offering any gift to God if we had hate in our hearts:

'If you are about to offer your gift to God at the altar and there you remember that your brother has something against you, leave your gift there in front of the altar, go at once and make peace with your brother, and then come back and offer your gift to God.' *(Matthew 5.23-24, GNB)*

Poem   How hard it is to offer him
the finest gifts we own:
our treasures and our secrets,
before the Baby's throne.

How hard it is to do our best
to live and work and play
as Jesus said his followers should,
   today and every day.

How hard it is to give ourselves —
our kindness, love and care;
but as we reach the Baby's throne
   we'll leave our gifts right there.

Prayer   Just as I am, young, strong, and free,
   To be the best that I can be
   For truth and righteousness and thee,
      Lord of my life, I come. *(Marianne Farningham)*

We can change

The Assembly

Preparation
Prepare four display cards to hold up by enlarging the sketches given below.

Talk
(Hold up card 1, side 1) What is this? A mouse, which might live in a cellar or a barn. That mouse is going to change ... *(turn the card over quickly)* ... into a horse. How handsome he is! He's nothing like the mouse! In the story of Cinderella some mice turned into horses, and drew her coach to the ball. They changed at the wave of a wand; but that was magic, in a fairy story.

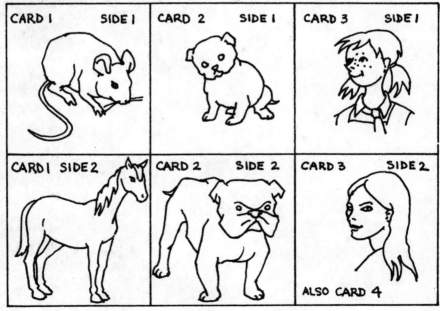

We shall look at something else that changes, in real life. *(Hold up card 2, side 1)* Here is a puppy, all warm and cuddly, lovely to play with. See what he'll change into. *(Turn the card over quickly)* It's not a monster — it's a bulldog: rather fat, rather ugly, and not a bit cuddly! And that's not a fairy story — it really happens. Not quickly, but gradually, over the years. The bulldog is still the same animal; he didn't change, like the mouse, into something different; he just grew up.

(Hold up card 3, side 1) Here's Amelia Agatha Jane. She's about ten. Look at her hair, untidy as usual; and her spotty face — but perhaps they're just freckles. She's not a very pretty sight! *(Turn the card over quickly)* Here she is ten years later. She's changed! Now she's really beautiful, with well-brushed hair and a lovely, smooth complexion. She, too, has grown up. But she's still the same person. When she was ten she was afraid of spiders; she still is. When she was ten she had an awful temper; she still has. But now look how she's changed. *(Hold up card 4, which is identical with card 3 side 2)*

You look puzzled; does she look just the same? She's not much older, certainly. A little while ago she thought she couldn't change. 'I was born with a bad temper and I've still got one. Don't blame me,' she said. 'That's what I'm supposed to be like — it's me.' But she did change; she changed herself, without a magic wand or a new hair-style, into a much nicer person.

There's a story in the Bible of a man who changed when he had met Jesus. Perhaps that's just what Amelia Agatha Jane did.

Reading

Listen to how this man changed when he met Jesus:

Jesus went on into Jericho and was passing through. There was a chief tax collector there named Zacchaeus, who was rich. He was trying to see who Jesus was, but he was a little man and could not see Jesus because of the crowd. So he ran ahead of the crowd and climbed a sycomore tree to see Jesus, who was going to pass that way. When Jesus came to that place, he looked up and said to Zacchaeus, 'Hurry down, Zacchaeus, because I must stay in your house today.'

Zacchaeus hurried down and welcomed him with great joy. All the people who saw it started grumbling, 'This man has gone as a guest to the home of a sinner!'

Zacchaeus stood up and said to the Lord, 'Listen, sir! I will give half my belongings to the poor, and if I have cheated anyone, I will pay him back four times as much.'

(Luke 19.1-8, GNB)

Alternative story: How Mr Brown changed

Mr Brown worked for a large taxi firm and earned a great deal of money. But he wasn't happy. Every day he saw many people who could never afford to ride in his firm's taxis. They looked tired and worried, and often the children were obviously hungry. He wished he could help. One day he sent £10 to a Children's Society. He had done something.

Months later he saw some children playing. They had no shoes on and he was afraid they would cut their feet. Perhaps his money hadn't been enough to buy them shoes, he thought. Without giving his name, he sent a larger sum of money to the Children's Society, and hoped he would feel happier.

But a week later he heard of a family living near him who hadn't been able to afford a holiday for six years. Perhaps his money still wasn't enough. What else could he do? He thought hard, then made a great decision.

'I've given them money,' he told his wife, 'but now I'm going to give myself.'

Mr Brown gave up his job. He and his wife moved away from their fine house into a tiny flat, and Mr Brown offered himself to the Children's Society.

'I would like to work for you,' he told the people there. 'I know you won't be able to pay me as much as I have been earning, but I would like to be able to change my life so that I can help the children I have seen suffering.'

The work was hard, and the pay was poor, but now Mr Brown was happy.

Reading

Paul wrote about changing oneself in his letter to the Christians in Ephesus:

Get rid of your old self, which made you live as you used to. Your hearts and minds must be made completely new, and you must put on the new self, which is created in God's likeness.

(Part of Ephesians 4.22-24, GNB)

Hymns

Give me joy in my heart
Reach out to your neighbour   (SM 22)
When a knight won his spurs

Prayer

We know, Father God, that we will change, quite naturally, as we grow older. We will grow taller and stronger; we will know more than we do now, and we will be able to do things that are impossible now. May we be ready for change, not only in our bodies but in our minds, so that we can grow up as your children, in wisdom and understanding.

Follow-up for the class-room

1 Make individual ladders out of folded paper. Beginning at the lowest rung, write the words WALKING and TALK-ING. Proceed up the ladder, writing on each step something that is learnt or achieved as you grow older, eg skipping, cycling, swimming, diving, etc.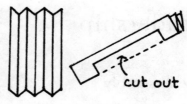

2 Make a series of pictures showing (a) egg, caterpillar, chrysalis, butterfly; and (b) frogspawn, tadpole, frog. The title could be THESE THINGS CHANGE — SO COULD I.

3 Read together how Saul changed on the way to Damascus: Acts 9.1-10, 17-19. Dramatise or illustrate. Write out what Paul later wrote in one of his letters to fellow-Christians: Ephesians 4, first part of verse 22.

Leadership

The Assembly

Story
For a long time the people of Israel had been hounded by their enemies, the Midianites. They had been forced to leave their homes and hide in burrows and caves in the wild country away from the towns. They longed to get back to the homes they loved, but the Midianites were everywhere. They ruined any crops the Israelites tried to grow and stole their animals. The Israelite people were close to starvation; they needed help, but who could lead them in attacking the Midianites? In desperation they cried to God, 'Help us! Help us!'

There was a young Israelite called Gideon. One day as he was secretly threshing wheat to provide food for his family, he noticed a stranger sitting under an oak tree nearby. The stranger moved nearer and began to speak. 'God is with you, brave and mighty man!' he said. Gideon had never thought of himself as brave or mighty before, and he was even more astonished when he heard the stranger telling him to use his strength and intelligence to lead his people in attacking the enemy.

'Me?' asked Gideon. 'How can *I* rescue all my people? My family isn't a powerful one amongst the Israelites, and I'm not even an important member of my family!'

'You *can* do it,' said the stranger, 'and you *will* do it — because God will help you. He will give you the power you need, the ideas, and men who will come forward to help you.'

It took a lot of thinking about. Often Gideon wondered if he had imagined his conversation with the stranger. Again and again he wanted God to give him proof that he really was the man chosen to lead the attack. But all the time ideas were beginning to form in his head about how, if he was the man, he would plan the onslaught. Would he do it with thousands of men, or merely a few hundred? Would they need to be fully armed? And how would the enemy react when he had finally decided upon the best moment to confront them?

Carefully Gideon noted the position of the enemy camps; they were huddled between the hills in the little valleys. He kept watch day by day, noticing how the troops were stationed and what their movements were. He crept among the rocks above the camps at night and watched while everything appeared to be quiet and still; the Midianites obviously did not expect to be attacked at night. They had only a few guards on duty then, not nearly enough to defend the whole army.

Secretly, Gideon rallied his troops, gathering the strongest and fittest men from the many Israelite tribes. He didn't realise there were so many — thousands of them met him at a secret rendezvous in the hills.

'I don't need that many,' thought Gideon, and realised that God was again guiding his thoughts. Gradually he selected a few hundred men, those who seemed the steadiest and most reliable. 'The time is nearly ready,' he told them, as he returned from a further reconnaissance of the camp sites.

One night everything seemed right for the attack, and Gideon was certain that God spoke to him. 'Get up and attack!' the voice said over and over again.

Dividing his chosen men into three groups, Gideon gave his instructions: 'Each man will be issued with a trumpet,' he told them, 'and each man should also carry a jar with a lighted flare-torch inside it.' Weapons were not going to be necessary for this night operation. 'You must creep to your positions, keeping to the hills on three sides of the enemy camp,' Gideon explained. 'Watch for my signal. When my men blow their trumpets, you must all blow yours. Then shout as loudly as you can, "For the Lord and for Gideon!" '

As the guards in the Midianite camp were changed that night, they little guessed what was to happen! The hills were as quiet and dark as usual, and the troops were sleeping peacefully. Suddenly the air seemed to explode with noise! All around them trumpets blasted, and great shouts of triumph came circling from the hills. Then the night sky blazed with light as the crash of breaking pottery revealed the lighted flares.

The whole Midianite camp sprang up in panic, the men frightened out of their sleep. They rushed this way and that, screaming and terrified. In the confusion the Midianite soldiers mistook their own troops for the enemy, thinking only that the camp had been invaded, and began killing each other with their swords.

Gideon's plan had succeeded: his surpise attack had frightened the enemy, and the men were fleeing for their lives. His leadership had been good, his strategy sound, and the Israelites were saved.

(Based on Judges 6—7)

Alternative talk

It might be possible to invite a blind person and his guide dog to the Assembly. If this can be arranged, and the person is willing to talk to the children, ask him to tell how the guide dog can lead him and keep him safe. Draw the analogy of the reliance on the guide dog being something like one's reliance upon God. Without the guide dog, life could be dangerous or hazardous for the blind person; without a trust in God as leader, life could be the same for us, even with our good sight.

Similarly, a vicar or minister might be called upon to talk about the guidance he received which determined his career. This could be followed by the statement that he is, in his church and in the community, a leader. He could be asked to tell how he thinks his own leadership of other people is important, and how he relies on God's guidance when making decisions.

Readings

If we say we follow God, we must expect to be led by him. He promises to help us know what is right, and to guide us so that we know what to do. In the book of the prophet Isaiah we are told that God says:

'I will lead my blind people
    by roads they have never travelled.
I will turn their darkness into light
    and make rough country smooth before them.
These are my promises,
    and I will keep them without fail.'

(Isaiah 42.16, GNB)

Jesus was a good leader, otherwise the disciples would not have left everything in order to follow him. He not only taught them with words, but was an example to them in the way he lived. He said that people had been told:

' "Love your neighbour, hate your enemy." But what I tell you is this: Love your enemies and pray for your persecutors; only so can you be children of your heavenly Father, who makes his sun rise on good and bad alike, and sends the rain on the honest and the dishonest. There must be no limit to your goodness, as your heavenly Father's goodness knows no bounds.'

Later, when Jesus was about to be killed, this is what happened:

There were two others with him, criminals who were being led away to execution; and when they reached the place called The Skull, they crucified him there, and the criminals with him, one on his right and the other on his left. Jesus said, 'Father, forgive them; they do not know what they are doing.'

(Matthew 5.43-45,48; Luke 23.32-34, NEB)

Prayers

Help us, O God, to recognise the people who are leaders in the world. Some of them are good and lead people in the ways you want. Others are leading along the wrong paths, away from you. May we be able to see what is right, and choose to follow only those who are willing to lead us in your direction.

Help those amongst us who are leaders, Father God. May we never use our power and influence to hurt others, however weak they may be, but to see, in ourselves, the power to do good at all times.

Hymns
Follow my leader   (SM 38)
Lead us, heavenly Father, lead us
O Jesus, I have promised

Follow-up for the class-room

1   Make a model, or draw maps and plans, of Gideon's attack on the Midianites. Parts of the story could be illustrated or dramatised.

2   List the attributes of a good leader, and discuss the findings.

3   Let the children imagine they are to form a club, or gang, or society. If they were the leader, what rules would they make, and why?

4   Design a badge, banner, or flag, which would represent, in the children's eyes, the Christian cause.

We choose

The Assembly

Preparation
Obtain a copy of *Which?* magazine

Talk
Have you seen one of these magazines? *(Hold up 'Which?')* Perhaps your parents sometimes have a copy to help them decide which new washing machine or toaster or hair drier to choose; or which new toy or bicycle to choose as a present for you. *Which?* gives them help and advice.

Right from babyhood we have to choose and select. It may be only 'Which toy shall I play with?' or 'Which colour shall I use to paint this picture?' or 'Which record shall I buy with my pocket money?' We shall go on making choices, all the time we are at school, and after we have left.

When a lady is going to buy a new dress she doesn't go into a shop and buy the first thing she sees. She has to choose what she can afford; she has to choose the colour that is most suitable for her and for the rest of her wardrobe; and she has to decide whether the material and design are right for the occasion on which she is going to wear the dress. She also has to decide whether the dress is well made and will therefore last well, and whether it is a good fit.

Every day on the roads we can see people making choices. Sometimes we see people at a crossroads studying a map; it is important for them to choose the right road. There are other decisions, too, like 'Can I get my car into that parking space?' or 'Shall I be able to pass that bus?' or 'Is it safe to cross the road now?' and so on. All the choices have to be made quickly; dithering might prove dangerous, and sometimes even fatal.

At some point we have to make a choice about what we are going to do when we leave school. It is a decision which doesn't usually have to be made quickly, like 'Shall I turn right or left?' Usually the choice is made gradually, after a lot of thought and consideration. The choice will depend on questions we ask ourselves, like 'What am I good at?' or 'What do I particularly enjoy doing?' or 'Am I prepared to go on studying in order to be better qualified in the end?' However long the thinking time, choose we must. Sometimes we may need to seek the help of other people, to advise us or to give us further information, but it is *our* choice in the end.

There's another choice which it is difficult to avoid, too. The choice of whether or not you will try to lead a Christian life, whether or not you will let Jesus be your leader. He will not choose for you, you are free to say 'No': the choice is yours. But think how much better, and how much easier, all your other choices will be if you know that you have chosen him — your friend for life.

Story

Simon the magician was popular. 'He's great!' said the people who lived in his town, and 'I'm great!' said Simon, as he performed his tricks and practised his magic. Every day he had an audience, from the most important citizens to the lowliest workers. He had been a magician for many years, but the people never tired of watching him. Some even believed he had the power of God.

One day, however, a man with a new kind of power came into the city. His name was Philip. Word went round quickly that he had been a friend of Jesus, the man of God who had been crucified in Jerusalem. Philip was soon gathering crowds of people round him. He told them about the kingdom of God, and he even healed people, just as Jesus had done.

Simon the magician watched and listened from a distance. He knew he was clever, and could earn good money by performing his magic; he knew his words were listened to; and he knew his spells could bring fear or comfort. But somehow he began to feel that this man Philip had something more, something that Simon wished he had himself. The crowds obviously felt Philip's magnetism, and they accepted his message, listening eagerly as he asked them to wash away all the wrong things in their lives, to begin again, following God in a new and exciting way. He asked them to believe that his way was the best, and he invited them to show their belief by being baptised.

Simon knew he had to make a choice. Either he could rush in, demanding by his miracles and his magic that the crowds should follow him, or he could become a follower himself, a servant of God.

And so it was that as the people of his town — men, women and young people — were immersed in water as a sign that they washed away their wrongs, Simon, too made his decision.

'Baptise me; I believe,' he said to Philip.

There was no going back; the choice had been made. Simon's magic and his popularity had been pushed aside for ever. From now on his place would be at Philip's side. Some of his ideas needed to be changed and his principles altered, but he was ready to begin a new life, he was ready to follow.

(Based on Acts 8.4-13)

Alternative story: Which jewel?

Gudron was a princess. She knew she was a princess because she lived in a palace, and because her father was a king and her mother a queen. In her wardrobe she had a crown — only a very small one — and every Thursday she took it out of its tissue paper wrapping and dusted it. There were six jewels in her crown, and each one was a different colour. On state occasions Gudron wore the crown so that the jewel right above her nose matched the colour of the dress she was wearing.

One day her mother, the queen, sent for her. 'Tomorrow you will be ten years old,' she said. Gudron didn't really need to be reminded; she had been counting the days to her birthday for a month, and today she was so excited that she hadn't eaten any breakfast. 'When you were a baby,' the queen went on, 'we had a very big party for you. That was when we gave you your name. People travelled from far away places just to see you, and they brought you presents: gold and silver and satin. There was one very special guest at that party, an old, old lady, who didn't bring any gift. She simply held you in her arms. "I'll come back in ten years," she said, "and you may choose your very own present." '

Gudron skipped about all day, thinking about the old lady. What present should she choose? A huge doll, with moving eyes and beautiful clothes? A gold bicycle? A pony of her own to ride in the palace grounds?

When she woke the next morning, the old lady was already in her bedroom, pulling back the heavy blue curtains so that the sunlight flooded in. Gudron rubbed her eyes and sat up. Was she still dreaming? The old lady had been to the wardrobe and unwrapped Gudron's little crown. The coloured jewels shone brightly in the daylight.

The old lady spoke. 'Each of these jewels represents a gift,' she said. 'You may choose just one of them. The red jewel stands for great wealth; choose that and you will never need to worry about money. The blue stone means you can have a room full of toys — dolls, books, games, puzzles, pictures — everything. And they will never become old or broken.' Gudron gasped; it was a lovely thought — toys for ever and ever, and as many as she could ever want!

The old lady continued, 'The green jewel will give you brains; it would make you very clever and wise.' Gudron smiled with pleasure: she would love to be so clever that she need never go to school again!

'Look at the yellow jewel,' said the old lady. 'That will provide you with friends: you will never be lonely, all through your life. And this purple jewel will give you long life and good health.' Gudron had once had measles. She remembered how unwell she had felt. It would be lovely never to feel ill or uncomfortable again.

'And this orange jewel,' the old lady was saying, 'this will give you a loving heart.' Gudron was hardly listening by now, and besides, a loving heart didn't sound very exciting. She had so much to choose from already.

'Must I decide at once?' she wanted to know.

'I'll come back again at sunset,' said her visitor. 'Think about it during the day, and you must choose tonight.' Suddenly she was gone — as silently as she had appeared.

At breakfast Gudron could think of nothing but a room full of toys. She imagined herself sitting in the middle of them, playing happily from morning until night. But, she thought, she would be forced to leave them sometimes to go to school — unless she chose the green jewel and became so clever that she could stay at home. Also, she thought, she would be grown up one day, and what would be the good of a room full of toys then?

She considered the red jewel, which stood for wealth: riches, gold and silver; a purse always full of money. But perhaps people would envy her so much that they would keep away from her. Or, worse still, they might only want to be friends with her for what she could give them.

At lunch time she thought about friends again: the yellow jewel would give her friends, boys and girls who would always want to play with her. They would be able to run races in the gardens, and tell each other secrets, and eat feasts together. But, Gudron considered, they would always be round at the palace asking her to play, and she often enjoyed being quite alone, to think, or plan, or read, or to play patience. Perhaps they would become nuisances instead of companions.

At supper time Gudron knew she would have to make her choice soon. What about good health and a long life? Would that really make her happy? She remembered Tappi, the little blind boy who lived in the town. He didn't seem to be unhappy even though he couldn't see. He laughed when he bumped into things and even thought it was a joke when he fell over. He was always happy. You didn't seem to need health to be happy.

As she got to her bedroom that night, Gudron still hadn't decided. Should she choose the red, blue, yellow, purple or green? But that was only five. What had the old lady said about the orange jewel? She couldn't remember. Well, in that case it couldn't have been very important.

'Gudron!' A voice behind her made her jump. It was the old lady, back again. She looked so old, so frail, so ill.

Gudron ran to her, holding out her arms. 'Do sit down,' she said. 'Let me get you a cup of tea, and a cushion.' And without waiting for an answer she ran off to find the things that would make the old lady comfortable.

'You've chosen well,' said the old lady when Gudron came back. Gudron stood still, puzzled. She hadn't decided yet; she still didn't know which gift to choose.

'What do you mean?' she asked.

'You have chosen the very best,' the old lady whispered. 'Toys, wealth, health, friends, brains — these things are not the most important, and they won't always make you happy. But a loving heart will be yours for always, and it will bring you great happiness. It will also make others happy, which means a great deal.'

Gudron remembered the orange jewel — the gift of a loving heart. Yes, she had chosen it; it was what she wanted most of all, and it had already started to work.

Readings

The woman in this story made a choice, and Jesus seemed to think it was a good one:

While they were on their way Jesus came to a village where a woman named Martha made him welcome in her home. She had a sister, Mary, who seated herself at the Lord's feet and stayed there listening to his words. Now Martha was distracted by her many tasks, so she came to him and said, 'Lord, do you not care that my sister has left me to get on with the work by myself? Tell her to come and lend a hand.' But the Lord answered, 'Martha, Martha, you are fretting and fussing about so many things; but one thing is necessary. The part that Mary has chosen is best; and it shall not be taken away from her.'

(Luke 10.38-42, NEB)

Simon Peter had to choose whether or not to follow Jesus. It may have been a difficult choice for him: he had a good job, a home and a family, and he would have to leave that behind if he went with Jesus. Jesus could not promise him wealth, or a home, but Peter believed that Jesus had something good to offer, and he was willing to give up his own comfort and security for Jesus. The other disciples must have felt the same. This is what happened:

As Jesus walked along the shore of Lake Galilee, he saw two fishermen, Simon and his brother Andrew, catching fish with a net. Jesus said to them, 'Come with me, and I will teach you to catch men.' At once they left their nets and went with him.

He went a little farther on and saw two other brothers, James and John, the sons of Zebedee. They were in their boat getting their nets ready. As soon as Jesus saw them, he called them; they left their father Zebedee in the boat with the hired men and went with Jesus.

(Mark 1.16-20, GNB)

Prayer

We know, Father God, that every day we have choices to make. Some of them do not matter much, others are important. Be with us as we choose. Help us always to think wisely, and to ask for your help and guidance.

Hymns
Lord of all hopefulness
One more step along the world I go   (CP 47)
Onward! Christian soldiers

Follow-up for the class-room

1   Ask the children to keep records of all personal choices they make during one day. These could be listed in two columns: *Choice* and *What I chose*.

2   By studying such biblical passages as Mark 1.14-20, Mark 2.13-14, and Luke 19.1-8, help the children to notice how often a personal meeting with Jesus leads to a decision. Look also at Luke 18.18-23, an 'unfinished' story, and discuss the rich man's choices and make suppositions as to what happened afterwards.

3   Begin to make a frieze, or a folding book, with pictures of the disciples under the heading *These men chose to follow Jesus*. In subsequent sessions you could examine how men and women through the ages (include some topical examples) have also chosen to follow him.

4   Write a diary that could have been kept by Simon the magician, showing how his life was changed by meeting Philip. Teachers should read on (Acts 8.18-24) to see how he had mistaken the meaning and role of Christian discipleship. This might be discussed with older scholars.

Darkness and light

The Assembly

Preparation
Prepare for this Assembly by keeping some cut flowers (or a pot plant) in the dark for at least five days.

Talk
Have any of you woken in the middle of the night and found yourselves in complete darkness? What did you do? Did anyone switch on the light, or find a torch? Did you feel happier, and safer, when you did that?

We all need light. What part of us tells us whether it is light or dark? When light enters our eyes we can see — light is necessary for sight.

Most living things are happier in the light, and some could not survive without it. *(Show flowers or plant)* Look at these flowers. They have been in the dark for several days. What has happened to them? They are faded and pale — they needed the light.

Some things, of course, can only begin life by staying in the dark: flower bulbs, or seeds. Most need the darkness beneath the soil to germinate properly. Baby gerbils, hamsters or mice grow for some time in complete darkness in their mother's body, just as you did before you were born. But when they are born, they — and you — need light.

People in Old Testament times believed that light was holy. And Jesus said of himself, 'I am the light of the world. No follower of mine shall wander in the dark; he shall have the light of life.' *(John 8.12, NEB)*

There was a time when Peter, one of Jesus' closest friends and followers, felt as though he was living in the dark. It was light outside, but he couldn't seem to see clearly. Even when the sun shone, it was like a day when low cloud hung everywhere, dark and heavy, promising rain. Peter knew exactly when it had started to seem dark, and he wished he could turn time backwards, so that the dreadful things of the past few weeks hadn't yet happened. Perhaps he could have prevented them happening.

It had been dark when it all began. They had walked across the valley to the

64

Mount of Olives after nightfall — Peter and his friends, and the leader of their group, Jesus. And it was there, in the dark, that Jesus had been arrested, and his friends had scattered. Perhaps Peter should have put up more of a fight. Perhaps he should have refused to leave Jesus' side, sharing with him the humiliation and indignity of the so-called trial. Instead, he had hidden, watching from a distance, and had told people that he was nothing to do with the prisoner, that he didn't even know him. Peter shuddered with shame at the thought. He wondered what would have happened if he had said, 'Yes, he's my best friend!' Jesus had been hung on that awful cross and died; Peter might well have been dead by now as well.

But Jesus wasn't dead — not now. He had actually come back and spoken to them all — they had seen him, and heard him, and eaten with him. Why then did Peter still feel as though everything were dark? Why did he feel so ashamed? His mind went back yet again to that little courtyard where he had said, 'I don't know him! I don't know what you're talking about!'

Now they had returned to Galilee. Peter was back with the people he had grown up with, and he was spending the night fishing; it was his old trade. He was glad to be on the boat again, and he was glad of the darkness.

But by the first light of morning he knew that the cloud had not lifted. The sun rose above the hills in a golden ball, and the lake steamed and shone, but Peter's own cloud was still there.

'Look!' shouted one of his friends in the fishing boat. 'There's a man down by the water's edge. He says we should cast the net to starboard and we'll make a catch. It's worth a try!'

They threw out the net, and caught so many fish that they couldn't haul it back in again.

Someone else cried out, 'It's Jesus!'

Peter didn't wait; he jumped from the boat into the water and struggled ashore. He emerged dripping wet and out of breath. Jesus stood there, ready with a charcoal fire to cook fish for breakfast.

Throughout the picnic meal Peter watched Jesus. Should he speak to him, admit he had let him down? Would that make this awful cloud of depression go away? Then after the meal Jesus moved closer to Peter, but the fisherman hardly dared to look up and meet his eyes.

'Do you love me?' asked Jesus.

'Of course I do!' said Peter in a whisper. Jesus didn't say a word about Peter running away, or pretending not to know him; he only wanted to be sure of one thing, of Peter's love.

'Then you must take care of my sheep,' Jesus said.

Peter suddenly knew that everything was all right. It was as if the cloud had lifted. He looked up, smiling as he had never smiled before, and he could see the sun, bright and blazing and clear again. He knew that Jesus had forgiven him, and still needed him. He would be Jesus' follower for life.

Readings
A follower of Jesus said:

God is light, and there is no darkness at all in him. If, then, we say that we have fellowship with him, yet at the same time live in the darkness, we are lying both in our words and in our actions. But if we live in the light — just as he is in the light — then we have fellowship with one another.

(1 John 1.5b-7a, GNB)

Jesus told his friends:

'You are like light for the whole world. A city built on a hill cannot be hidden. No no lights a lamp and puts it under a bowl; instead he puts it on the lampstand, where it gives light for everyone in the house. In the same way your light must shine before people, so that they will see the good things you do and praise your Father in heaven.'

(Matthew 5.14-16, GNB)

Prayer
In your light, Lord Jesus, let us live. Under your light may we work and play and, by sharing your light, may we shine for other people.

Hymns
From the darkness came light   (CP 29)
Morning has broken
Ye holy angels bright

Music
Gershwin: Rhapsody in Blue (Piano Concerto) — Opening theme.

Follow-up for the class-room

1   Grow cress seeds, keeping one pot in the dark and the other in the light, and noting the results over a period of ten days or so.

2   Make a survey of lighting through the ages, and the fuel and power used to create light.

3   Examine such phrases as 'It dawned on me', 'I was in the dark', 'I've seen the light' etc, to see how solutions to problems are like going into the light again. Link this if possible with the story of the two friends on the road to Emmaus: Luke 24.13-35.

What are we doing?

The Assembly

Preparation

You will need a large picture showing a wood or a forest; and smaller pictures of birds, including an owl; and deer, squirrels and mice. Also illustrations of ivy, acorns or nuts, leaves, toadstools or fungi, insects and grubs. These should be large enouth to be seen by all; display each as you speak about it.

Talk

Have you ever realised just how organised our world is? Even a wood or forest is a separate unit, a living community, with each thing living in it dependent on something else for survival or reproduction.

Here is a wood; you *could* walk through it and see only trees, huge and sturdy. But you *should* be able to see other things as well: birds, for instance. Many of them have nests up there in the branches, protected by the leaves and by their high position. The birds themselves live by eating insects and grubs which live amongst the trees: on the barks, or on the leaves, or on the ground between the trees. Sometimes you may see, or hear, an owl. He lives here, too, feeding on mice and other small creatures.

These deer depend on the woodland for their diet. They eat the young branches and saplings. Squirrels eat the acorns and other nuts, and the mice eat the seeds and sometimes the grubs in the ground.

The tree is also the home for the ivy plant which clings round its trunk and branches, relying on them for support and nourishment. The tree's own leaves fall to the ground; next time you are in a wood look at the forest floor and you will see layer upon layer of dead leaves. These are gradually pushed down into the earth, where they make the soil rich and present the right condition for germinating the trees' seeds which also fall. Sometimes, too, we can see toadstools and fungi in a wood; and these also are dependent on the trees for their existence.

Without the trees other plants would not be able to grow, nor animals to survive. How well it has all been planned!

Readings

This psalm is full of praise for God who planned the earth in such detail and with such care:

You created the moon to mark the months;
  the sun knows the time to set.
You made the night, and in the darkness
  all the wild animals come out.
The young lions roar while they hunt,
  looking for the food that God provides.
When the sun rises, they go back
  and lie down in their dens.
Then people go out to do their work
  and keep working until evening.
Lord, you have made so many things!
  How wisely you made them all!
  The earth is filled with your creatures.
There is the ocean, large and wide,
  where countless creatures live,
  large and small alike.
All of them depend on you
  to give them food when they need it.
You give it to them, and they eat it;
  you provide food, and they are satisfied.

I will sing to the Lord all my life;
  as long as I live I will sing praises to my God.

(Psalm 104.19-25,27-28,33, GNB)

God knows all about us, and we cannot hide from him. This beautiful psalm of praise was written thousands of years ago, but God never changes:

Lord, you have examined me
  and you know me.
You know everything I do;
  from far away you understand all my thoughts.
You see me, whether I am working or resting;
  you know all my actions.
Even before I speak,
  you already know what I will say.
You are all round me on every side;
  you protect me with your power.
Your knowledge of me is too deep;
  it is beyond my understanding.

69

You created every part of me;
  you put me together in my mother's womb.
I praise you because you are to be feared;
  all you do is strange and wonderful.
  I know it with all my heart.
When my bones were being formed,
  carefully put together in my mother's womb,
when I was growing there in secret,
  you knew that I was there —
  you saw me before I was born.

(Psalm 139.1-6,13-16a, GNB)

The Hebrew people always remembered that God had created them and everything around them. They pictured him triumphantly and lovingly bringing the world together, a unit of existence, with everything having a place and a purpose:

Then God said, 'Let the earth produce fresh growth, let there be on the earth plants bearing seed, fruit-trees bearing fruit each with seed according to its kind.' So it was; and God saw that it was good.

God said, 'Let there be lights in the vault of heaven to separate day from night, and let them serve as signs both for festivals and for seasons and years. Let them also shine in the vault of heaven to give light on earth.' So it was; God made the two great lights, the greater to govern the day and the lesser to govern the night; and with them he made the stars. And God saw that it was good.

God said, 'Let the waters teem with countless living creatures, and let birds fly above the earth across the vault of heaven.' God then created the great sea-monsters and all living creatures that move and swarm in the waters, according to their kind, and every kind of bird; and God saw that it was good.

God said, 'Let the earth bring forth living creatures, according to their kind: cattle, reptiles, and wild animals, all according to their kind.' So it was; God made wild animals, cattle, and all reptiles, each according to its kind; and he saw that it was good.

(Part of Genesis 1.11-25, NEB)

Prayer
Father God, you have given us this world to be our home. Help us to realise how much we rely upon it for our existence: on plants, animals and minerals. You planned the world's variety and beauty; help us to appreciate it and to take care of it, for we must pass it on, unspoiled, to our children.

Hymns
All creatures of our God and King
For the beauty of the earth
The earth is yours, Lord   (CP 6)

Music
Vaughan Williams: Fantasia on 'Greensleeves'.
Haydn: Chorus 'The Heavens are telling' from Creation.

Follow-up for the class-room

1   Seeing colour in God's wonderful world; using one colour at a time, make
a collage, cutting scraps of the chosen colour from magazines and wallpaper.
Glue them in a pattern on a piece of plain paper. Notice the variety of shades
within that colour.

2   Make a picture of a food chain, eg from humans to grass (through the
cow), or humans to plankton (through the fish).

3   Study how bees need flowers and flowers need bees, each being
dependent on the other. Follow this up by noting how we, as humans, are
dependent on other forms of life, and on each other.

4   Write about or make a wall picture of how God's world can be spoiled, eg
by smoke, poisonous chemicals, air pollution, dumped rubbish, graffiti,
unsightly architecture, etc.

5   List ways in which children can help to keep the world pure and clean;
perhaps a 'clean-up' campaign could be started in the class or in the school
which could lead to a general awareness of what is happening in the
community.

6   Prepare an Assembly to follow on from this one. Choose hymns, make up
a prayer, and prepare and rehearse the following talk and readings. You will
need newspaper and magazine cuttings as described below, two pairs of dark
glasses, and papers with the readings for the children written out.

Leader reads again Genesis 1.11-25 (see page 70). 'God saw that it was good' ...
and, having created the world, God created man to live in it.

71

Child reads Genesis 1.26-31, preferably from the New English Bible, ending at 'it was very good'.

Leader   'God saw all that he had made, and it was very good': would he think that it is good now, I wonder?

Children read reports of oil pollution, flooding of valleys, endangered animal species, child or animal abuse, vandalism, etc. These should be as topical and local as possible, so that everyone can be aware that the spoiling of life is close at hand.

Leader   Sometimes we say that people who see only the pleasant things in the world are looking through 'rose-tinted spectacles'. Two children are going to look at things through 'grey-tinted spectacles' and tell us what they see.

Two children put on dark glasses, and read from their prepared papers.

First child   I can see a boy and girl walking through a park. They have bought cans of Coke and some crisps. They are eating and drinking as they walk. They screw the crisp packets into balls and toss them into the bushes. They throw the empty cans on the ground, and kick them around until they are tired of it. Then they walk on, leaving the empty cans on the path.

Leader   'I never do that!' you say; but I know two other children who *do* leave litter about. The boy — we'll call him Billy — swears a lot, and his words fall like litter for younger boys and girls to pick up. The girl — she can be called Rose — is selfish: she always wants the best things for herself, and everywhere she goes she litters the place with her greed and selfishness.

Second child   I can see a boy and girl sitting on the top deck of a bus. One has a lipstick and the other a thick felt-tip pen. They think no one is looking, but I can see them. They are scrawling messages on the backs of the seats.

Leader   'I never do that!' you say, and perhaps you are right. But there are some children I know who spoil people's property by what they say. 'That's a dreadful model!' they might say. 'Mine is much better!' Or, 'You're so ugly it hurts me to look at you!' People who talk like that are leaving messages of unkindness everywhere.

What are we doing to God's world? Are we really caring for it as we should? Are we really much better than the vandals, the litter-louts, the destroyers and the spoilers?

Forgiving

The Assembly

Preparation
The story could be adapted for dramatisation if desired.

Story: How to forgive
Sir Arthur Markham was a very rich man. He had made his money by sheer hard work over many, many years. He had bought workshops and warehouses, and now he owned a big canning factory in a large industrial town. He planned to expand his business, which was doing very well, and needed to spend some time abroad, hoping to find new markets for his products. First, though, he had to engage a good manager for his factory here.

After interviewing several likely men, Sir Arthur appointed one who seemed to be the most promising. Together they drew up a contract setting out the terms, and the rules by which the factory was to be run. It was up to the new manager to employ new men as he needed them, and he was to be in complete charge.

At the end of the first year, Sir Arthur sent a representative to the factory to see how things were going, and to examine the firm's books to check the profits that were due to him. Sir Arthur couldn't have guessed what would happen: the man he sent was refused entry to the factory, and was even beaten up when he tried a second time! The new manager of the factory smiled to himself. He would take over, by force if necessary, Sir Arthur's rights to his shares in the business. He would not only run the factory *his* way, he would own it.

Sir Arthur couldn't understand it. Perhaps thugs had caught his representative unawares, and perhaps the manager had not been told about the mugging. In any case, he needed to know what was going on, and so he sent another man. A week or so later, Sir Arthur received reports that this man, too, had been mugged. Now he was definitely suspicious that the new manager and his workers were involved; it looked as though they had decided to take over the factory and keep all the profits for themselves.

73

Choosing the strongest man he knew, Sir Arthur sent him to the factory to attempt to gain entry. Somehow the criminals working there had to be exposed. But the same thing happened, only this time the man he had sent died later in hospital. It looked so much like an accident that it would be difficult to prove it wasn't, in a court of law; but Sir Arthur knew what must have happened.

'There's one person left,' he thought, 'the only man who can be really effective. I'll send my own son — they won't dare touch him.'

Sir Arthur's son was young and strong, and would be a good match for any muggers. He was also likeable, and fair; surely the men would respect him!

Sir Arthur waited anxiously for news, and when it came he was shattered. The manager and his men had been prepared for another visit, and when Sir Arthur's son arrived he was beaten up and horribly wounded. This time, if he died, it would certainly look like murder.

For hours Sir Arthur's son lay barely conscious. And then, leaning over him, one of the doctors at the hospital heard him say, 'Father, forgive them!'

This story could almost have been the story of God and his world, put into modern terms. When things were going wrong with his people in the world, God sent prophets and preachers and great leaders to persuade them to do the right things; but they were not accepted nor listened to. At last, God sent his son, Jesus, to show men the right way to live. But he, too, was killed; before he died, he said, 'Father, forgive them!'

Alternative story: No revenge

It was during the second world war that a soldier called Captain James Lees was sent on active service to an island near Greece. One day he found himself in a hand-to-hand fight with an Italian soldier, one of the enemy troops. Both men were equally well-equipped, and each was as strong as the other. In the fight they were both seriously wounded and taken to the same military hospital, where they lay side by side in the ward. A German doctor dressed their wounds, and an Italian nurse looked after them. For nearly a week doctor and nurse fought to save the soldiers' lives. But James Lees died, and the Italian soldier began to recover. His name was Roberto Commoti.

Quickly the news of James Lees' death reached his home in Dorset, and his family and friends, and all the people in the village where he had lived, were very sad. The hospital authorities had sent word to James' mother about the hand-to-hand battle he had had with Roberto Commoti, and had told her how James had died while the Italian lived.

Lady Lees, James' mother, was determined to go and find Roberto as soon as she could. She wasn't the sort of person who wanted revenge on the man who had killed her son; instead her heart was full of compassion for him because he, too, had suffered in the terrible war. She knew that what he had done had been forced upon him by being involved as a soldier, and that in times of peace he and her son could easily have been friends. Long before she found him she had forgiven him for the killing, and when at last she traced him they became close friends. It was almost as if he took the place of her son.

The story of Lady Lees was reported in the Italian newspapers, and the people of Italy were amazed at this brave and forgiving English woman. They were so impressed by her forgiving spirit that they awarded her a gold medal.

Readings

(The first reading is suitable for use following the story of Sir Arthur Markham.)
Jesus often taught people by telling them stories. Does this one remind you of the story you have just heard?

'There was once a man who planted a vineyard, let it out to tenants, and then left home for a long time. When the time came to gather the grapes, he sent a slave to the tenants to receive from them his share of the harvest. But the tenants beat the slave and sent him back without a thing. So he sent another slave; but the tenants beat him also, treated him shamefully, and sent him back without a thing. Then he sent a third slave; the tenants wounded him, too, and threw him out. Then the owner of the vineyard said, "What shall I do? I will send my own dear son; surely they will respect him!" But when the tenants saw him, they said to one another, "This is the owner's son. Let's kill him and his property will be ours!" So they threw him out of the vineyard and killed him.'

(Luke 20.9-15, GNB)

Here are a few verses from the Bible about the death of Jesus:

They kept on shouting at the top of their voices that Jesus should be crucified, and finally their shouting succeeded. So Pilate passed the sentence on Jesus that they were asking for.

Two other men, both of them criminals, were also led out to be put to death with Jesus. When they came to the place called 'The Skull', they crucified Jesus there, and the two criminals, one on his right and the other on his left. Jesus said, 'Forgive them, Father! They don't know what they are doing.'

It was about twelve o'clock when the sun stopped shining and darkness covered the whole country until three o'clock; and the curtain hanging in the Temple was torn in two. Jesus cried out in a loud voice, 'Father! In your hands I place my spirit!' He said this and died.

(Luke 23.23-24,32-34,44-46, GNB)

75

Jesus always taught people that they must forgive. On one occasion he said,

'If your brother wrongs you, reprove him; and if he repents, forgive him. Even if he wrongs you seven times in a day and comes back to you seven times saying, "I am sorry", you are to forgive him.'

(Luke 17.3-4, NEB)

Hymns
Father, we thank thee for the night
Father, hear the prayer we offer
Heavenly Father, may thy blessing   (CP 62)

Prayer
Lord, we find it hard to forgive people, even when we know they are sorry. Help us to remember how other people have been able to forgive great wrongs, and how Jesus Christ was able to say 'Forgive them' even when he was dying. Make us kind and generous and loving, so that, in a small way, we may become more like you.

Follow-up for the class-room

1   Find out what the children regard as 'wrongs' done to them. Do they forgive? What do they mean by forgiving? Is the act of forgiveness merely words, or can they begin to see that it also means forgetting wholeheartedly? Ask them to write about a situation in which they could forgive someone, or a time when they have been forgiven by someone else.

2   From Bibles or the blackboard, copy these verses and decorate.
   You are good to us and forgiving,
      full of constant love for all who pray to you.
   You are mighty and do wonderful things;
      you alone are God.
(Psalm 86.5,10, GNB)

3   Ask the children to look in comics and cut out examples of people taking revenge. Make a collage of them with a large question 'Is revenge right?' as a caption. Discuss the situations in groups as the examples are found.

I do believe

The Assembly

Preparation

For the experiments you will need: (1) a piece of wood about 60 cms (2 ft) long, 5 cms (2 ins) wide, 2.5 cms (1 in) thick; a piece of broomstick. (2) a piece of wood about 120 cms (4 ft) long, 10 cms (4 ins) wide, 2.5-5 cms (1-2 ins) thick; a block of wood about 5 cms x 5 cms (2 ins x 2 ins), 15 cms (6 ins) long; three bricks.

Experiments

Use either or both experiments to demonstrate seeing and believing. For experiment (1) choose two pupils, one large and heavy, and the other as small as possible. Ask them to come to the front and talk for a few moments about their sizes and the fact that, normally, strength is relative to one's size and body weight. Say you will now prove that this is not necessarily so. Lay the wood flat on a table where all can see it. Ask the bigger pupil to press on one end of it with all his strength. Ask the smaller pupil to try to lift the other end; he should be unable to do so.

Now rest the wood centrally on the broomstick like a see-saw. The larger pupil should press one end of the wood down on to the table, and the smaller child should try again. He or she will probably still find it difficult or impossible to lift.

Then explain that you will show that the smaller pupil *can* lift the other's hands from the table, using only the wood and the broomstick. Move the broomstick so that it is only about 10 cms (4 ins) from one end of the wood. The bigger pupil should again press on the wood at the shorter end; invite the smaller child to try again. This time he should be able to lift the wood; he will appear to have become the stronger.

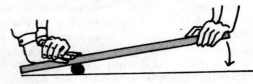

For experiment (2) have the three bricks in a pile on a table. Ask a pupil to try to lift the pile. It will either be impossible or very difficult, depending on the size of the child. Now ask if there is anyone who thinks they could lift them with only one finger. Select a fairly small child; ask him or her to come to the front, and ask if anyone believes that the chosen child could do it.

Set up the plank of wood on the small block of wood, so that the small block becomes the fulcrum, about 30 cms (12 ins) from one end. Put the pile of bricks on 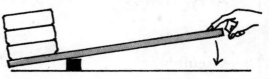 the shorter end of the plank, and invite the child to press on the other end with one finger. This should lift the bricks from the table.

Comment that no one believed the child could do it but having seen it they now believed it was possible.

Talk

Recall briefly that the disciples, after watching Jesus die, met together in secret, in the very depths of despair. The man on whom they had pinned their hopes and their beliefs had been murdered, in front of them, and none of them had been brave enough to try to save him. Perhaps some of them remembered him saying that the Son of Man would be handed over to men who would kill him, and perhaps they recalled, rather hopelessly, his words that three days later he would rise to life. But what could they believe now? They had *seen* him die.

Then, suddenly, he was with them again; he was real, he was alive! And, they believed. Trying to convince others, of course, was a problem. 'You're mad,' they said. 'We don't believe it!' But the disciples were absolutely certain: they had seen it with their own eyes.

Reading

The friends of Jesus were still shocked by the death of their leader. They dared not go out into the town, and were meeting secretly. It was still too soon for them to begin to decide what to do next.

It was late that Sunday evening, and the disciples were gathered together behind locked doors, because they were afraid of the Jewish authorities. Then Jesus came and stood among them. 'Peace be with you,' he said. The disciples were filled with joy at seeing the Lord.

One of the twelve disciples, Thomas, was not with them when Jesus came. So the other disciples told him, 'We have seen the Lord!'

Thomas said to them, 'Unless I see the scars of the nails in his hands, I will not believe.'

A week later the disciples were together again indoors, and Thomas was with them. The doors were locked, but Jesus came and stood among them and said, 'Peace be with you.' Then he said to Thomas, 'Put your finger here, and look at my hands. Stop your doubting, and believe!'

Thomas answered him, 'My Lord and my God!'

Jesus said to him, 'Do you believe because you see me? How happy are those who believe without seeing me!'

(Part of John 20.19-20,24-29, GNB)

Talk and story

Jesus said, 'How happy are those who believe without seeing me!' Down through two thousand years people the world over have come to believe that Jesus was the person they wanted to follow. Because he cared for others, and wanted to serve them, they too have wanted to serve and to care, knowing that Jesus has promised to be there to help. Often they themselves are surprised by the way their lives are altered by their decisions to help other people. One such person was Danilo Dolci.

One of the ways of becoming wealthy in any country is to become a well-qualified architect who can design good, modern buildings. Danilo Dolci, an Italian, decided he would earn his money by doing just that. As he was clever and hardworking, he soon completed his training and set out to become well-known. Danilo was also a Christian, with a firm belief that God would lead him and use him in some way.

At the beginning of his career, however, he never thought that God would expect him to give up what he was best at — designing buildings. But one day Danilo Dolci heard that in a village on the island of Sicily, just off the 'toe' of Italy, lived the poorest people imaginable.

'I must see them for myself,' he thought, and set off to travel to the village of Trappeto.

There he saw men, women and children wandering in the streets begging for food. There was no work for the grown-ups, and men crowded hopelessly and miserably together, wondering how to support their families. Danilo, remembering how Jesus had cared for poor and hopeless people, gave up all thoughts of going back to his own city and becoming a rich and famous architect.

'I'll stay here and help the people,' he said.

The first thing he noticed was that travelling between the villages in the remote parts of Sicily was difficult. The cart tracks filled with mud when it rained, and in the hot summers they were cracked and uneven.

'We'll rebuild the roads,' Danilo told the men. At least it would give them

79

useful work, for he knew how unemployment could make people desperately unhappy.

Government officials soon heard rumours of the road-building, and went to see what was going on.

'Who told you to organise this?' they asked Danilo.

'No one. But the men needed to have work to do,' said Danilo.

The officials were angry. 'But we didn't authorise it,' they said. 'You will be punished for not asking our permission.'

The police were sent to arrest Danilo and the road builders, and they found themselves thrown into prison.

Many people believed that, at the end of his prison sentence, Danilo would return to Italy convinced that he could do nothing for the people of Trappeto. But Danilo was still sure that they mattered, that each one of them was important, and he would not give up.

'Now if there was a better system of irrigation,' he thought, 'the people could make their farms produce better crops, and there would be more food for everyone.'

He persuaded the Government to use men from the village to build a dam, but once again the work was stopped unexpectedly after a few months, and the people began to suffer as they had before. This time, to show the Government how serious he was, Danilo decided to go on hunger strike. After he had gone without food for nine days, the Government at last gave in, frightened that Danilo would starve to death; the men were allowed to start work again.

Roads were rebuilt and the dam was made. The people at last earned more money, and were able to grow more crops, which saved them from their previous terrible poverty.

Danilo is still working for the poor people of Sicily and Italy, providing work for the unemployed, homes for the homeless, and medical aid for the sick.

'Jesus cared for everyone,' he says, 'and he wants us to care for each other in the same way.'

Hymns
Christ the Lord is risen today
Go, tell it on the mountain
Lord of the dance

Prayer
Thank you, dear Lord Jesus, for showing yourself to your friends. They believed you were alive, and began to pass on the message of Easter. Because

they were so sure that you had conquered death they were able to begin the great work of spreading the good news, and it is through them that we know and love you today.

Music
Schumann: Symphony No 1 (Spring) — opening of first movement.
Mahler: Symphony No 2 (The Resurrection).

Follow-up for the class-room

1   We believe because we see; make lists which bear this out. For example, when we see buds on the trees we believe spring is coming. Let the children do their own experiments to show that, for instance, seeds will not grow without moisture. These discoveries should be added to the lists.

2   Discuss how blind people learn to believe things they cannot see. This could lead on to the children believing without seeing, eg facts of history and geography, reported news items.

3   Tell the story of Saul, hater of the Christians, who spent a long time pursuing and persecuting them. Read together the story of how he came to believe in the risen Christ, and how that belief changed his whole life. (See Acts 8.1-3; 9.1-11,17-22.)

4   Start a project in which the children do something to help spread the story of Jesus; a Bible story scrap book could be made and given to a children's home; a new hymn learnt and sung to the rest of the school; a local church might need support for a missionary; a correspondence might be started with someone living or working with people of the third world.

Seeing God

The Assembly

Story: The school outing

It was a special bus that took the classes to the zoo. Some shoppers thought it was an ordinary bus, and held out their hands at the bus stops to ask the driver to pull up. But it was just full of children, all laughing and joking, and speculating on what they would see at the zoo.

Miss Day had told them all to bring a packed lunch, and also a notebook so that they could jot down the names of the animals and birds that they thought particularly funny, or beautiful, or clever. They could make drawings of them, too, and later would be able to make class-room friezes of all they had seen.

Suzanne and Jill had planned to keep together all day; Jill had a watch that would tell them when it was time to meet the others for lunch. They tumbled out of the bus together.

'Look,' said Suzanne almost as soon as they had gone through the entrance gates. 'There are the sea-lions; let's go and watch them. Can you hear them? They sound like dogs barking!'

Sleek and graceful, the sea-lions nosed through the water, then heaved themselves onto the rocks, swaying and snorting before diving back into the water.

Next to the sea-lions were the bears, padding heavily backwards and forwards; and near them the camels, in their own grassy paddock. One ambled over to the high fence and looked haughtily down at Jill and Suzanne.

'He's not very pretty, is he?' said Jill. 'His hair's falling out, too.'

They passed the kangaroos, sitting on their tails as they looked at the visitors, then suddenly dipping down into the long grass as their short front legs searched for food.

'What are all those people looking at?' asked Suzanne, seeing quite a crowd round one of the buildings.

Jill stood on tiptoe. A mynah bird laughed and shrieked, mocking the crowd, and everyone rocked with pleasure. 'It's the tropical bird house,' said Jill. 'It's too crowded there. Let's find something else.'

But Suzanne wanted to push her way through the crowds. Birds were her favourites. 'Come on,' she said. 'Let's just peep at them.'

So the girls pushed their way in. Suzanne gazed at the walls where the cages were set. Daylight shone through the glass roof making them look larger and very colourful. The noise in the building was sweet yet piercing, a great cloud of bird-song and chatter. Suzanne stopped in front of the first cage window; dozens of finches darted about, or perched, gossipping, in little huddles on the branches. Jill had gone on ahead, glancing at the birds as she hurried from cage to cage.

'Come on, Suzanne,' she said. 'I'm bored with birds. Let's go and find the monkeys.'

'You go on,' Suzanne replied. 'I haven't seen these properly yet.'

Jill disappeared into the crowds that were still round the mynah bird's cage. Suzanne moved on to another cage and read the label in front of her. 'Great bird of Paradise,' she read, 'from Papua New Guinea.' She couldn't move, and she hardly breathed. Here was the most beautiful thing she had ever seen! It was so brightly coloured; its beak and chin were a glossy greenish-black, and a dark green plume rose from the top of its head. From behind this plume, as far as its tail, shone the brightest yellow, and great flame-coloured feathers rose like a fountain of soft fire from behind its wings, swirling and swaying as it moved along the perch. Two long thin feather strands fell from its tail like trails of black ink. The tips of its wings were chestnut coloured, and its eyes were like bright amber beads.

'You beautiful, beautiful creature,' whispered Suzanne. She could hardly bear to take her eyes off it. She felt like singing, or laughing, or shouting out loud — surely everyone else had noticed that this bird house was somehow very special?

She became aware of Jill's voice calling, 'Suzanne, are you still in there? It's time to go and meet the others for lunch.' Suzanne left the bird house in a dream. Jill rattled on, 'I've had a great time; I've seen the monkeys, and the zebras, and a huge black gorilla!'

Suzanne was still thinking of the great bird of paradise. 'But I think I have seen God!' she said.

Alternative story: Is God real?

Martin and Sara went to a large school on the outskirts of a town. They were twins, and were in a class together. One day there was quite a long class discussion, during which Martin admitted that he believed in God. Many children in the class also believed, but they were not brave enough to admit it. They thought Martin would get teased. Sure enough, in the playground later, the teasing began.

'Hey, Martin!' called one of the boys. 'Go on then, make God do a miracle!'

Martin turned away and joined Sara, who was looking upset. 'That girl laughed at me,' she said. 'She said that if I believed in God I could get him to make me stand on my head. She knows I can't do that!'

'Come on, you two,' shouted another boy, laughing. 'Just tell that school to disappear! God will help!'

Martin and Sara hurried off. They didn't know what to think. 'Perhaps we are silly to believe in God,' said Martin. 'But how can we be sure?'

'Let's ask Grandad,' said Sara. 'He knows everything.'

Grandad was old and wise. He often gave the twins help with their homework, or answered their questions, or gave advice when they asked him. When he saw them after school that day, they looked really worried.

'What's up?' he asked them.

'Grandad, is God real?' Sarah said immediately. Grandad didn't say anything for a long time. Martin was half afraid he was going to say 'No'. Grandad went into the hall.

'Come for a walk, and we can find out,' he said. The twins were surprised: they hadn't expected that.

They went across the road and through the park gates. Most of the people had already gone home to tea, and it was quiet. Sara saw a squirrel balancing along the top of a fence. Birds fluttered in and out of a hedge. Grandad gently moved a few twigs in the hedge aside with his stick.

'Look in there,' he whispered. 'I noticed it yesterday when I was out walking.'

Sara and Martin peeped in. Deep inside the hedge a mother bird sat on her nest. She looked warily at the twins, but didn't move.

'Now, who taught her to look after her chicks so well?' asked Grandad. He bent down and picked a buttercup, yellow and glistening in the afternoon sun. They looked into it, and the twins noticed its soft crown of stamens, furry with pollen.

'Who could have made anything so beautiful?' whispered Sara.

At the other end of the park, great pylons reached into the sky, supporting an intricate pattern of cables.

'And Martin, who gave man a mind, so that he could discover electricity and learn to use it?' Grandad asked.

Martin could hear the drone of an aircraft, and spotted the silver giant high up in the blue sky. 'Or gave man a mind to invent great machines that would fly like birds?' he added.

Turning back into the town, the three of them passed a church. Grandad pointed to a crucifix in the churchyard. 'And who loved us enough to send his Son to show us how to live?' he asked quietly.

Martin and Sara were quite sure about God now.

'When you have any doubts about God,' Grandad said, 'just look around you. He is everywhere!'

Prayer

Thank you, God, for showing yourself to us in unexpected places. Keep our eyes and hearts ready for moments of great joy or beauty, so that we can recognise your hidden face and give you praise.

Readings

One of the song writers of the book of Psalms composed this great lyric of praise:

All you that are righteous,
  shout for joy for what the Lord has done;
  praise him, all you that obey him.
Give thanks to the Lord with harps,
  sing to him with stringed instruments.
Sing a new song to him,
  play the harp with skill, and shout for joy!

The words of the Lord are true
  and all his works are dependable.
The Lord loves what is righteous and just;
  his constant love fills the earth.
The Lord created the heavens by his command,
  the sun, moon, and stars by his spoken word.

May your constant love be with us, Lord,
  as we put our hope in you.

(Psalm 33.1-6,22, GNB)

In the Bible there is a collection of love poems, and one of these has this lovely description of springtime:

For now the winter is past,
the rains are over and gone;
the flowers appear in the country-side;
the time is coming when the birds will sing,
and the turtle-dove's cooing will be heard in our land;
when the green figs will ripen on the fig-trees
and the vines give forth their fragrance.

(Song of Songs 2.11-13a, NEB)

Hundreds of years before Jesus was born the Israelites loved to sing in praise of God. Sometimes they would form great processions, and sing accompanied by musical instruments. This is one of the songs they sang:

O come, let us sing unto the Lord: let us make a joyful noise to the rock of our salvation.

Let us come before his presence with thanksgiving, and make a joyful noise unto him with psalms.

For the Lord is a great God, and a great King above all gods.

In his hand are the deep places of the earth: the strength of the hills is his also.

The sea is his, and he made it: and his hands formed the dry land.

O come, let us worship and bow down: let us kneel before the Lord our maker.

For he is our God; and we are the people of his pasture, and the sheep of his hand.

(Psalm 95.1-7, AV)

Hymns
All creatures of our God and King
Praise, my soul, the King of heaven
Who put the colours in the rainbow?   (CP 12)

Music
Saint-Saens: Organ Symphony No 3 — opening of Adagio.
Mendelssohn: Symphony No 5 (Reformation) — Fourth movement.
Vaughan Williams — setting of the Old Hundredth.

Follow-up for the class-room

1   Try to show a picture of a great bird of paradise. Enlarge the one given here in outline, and use it for a class collage. It could be decorated with strips of coloured tissue paper, glitter, real feathers, foil, etc. Pictures of other tropical birds could be available, and a whole 'aviary' made for class-room display.

2   Ask the children to draw or write about the most beautiful thing they have ever seen.

3   Point out that people see God in different things, and not always in things of great beauty; for example, some recognise him through a knowledge of earth's forces in some branches of science. Other indications or signs of God would be seen by some people in the stained glass windows and majestic architecture of a great cathedral, in the swirling mist on a lonely moor, in a handful of shells at the seaside, in the swell of music, or the scent of a rose. If the children could show someone else God, how would they choose to do it? Write or discuss.

Unconditional love

The Assembly

Preparation
Arrange children so that there is a passageway down the centre of the hall. Have ready a bag full of 'money' or a wallet full of 'notes'. You will also need a ring, to denote prosperity, and a neat pile of boy's clothing: jacket, jersey and shoes.

Talk
We're going to act a story today. First we need a very rich man. *(Select a child to come to the front)* We know he's rich because he looks well-fed and smart. *(Put a ring on his finger)* He has lots of possessions, like this ring, and lots of money in the bank. *(Place bag of money or wallet on a table behind him)* He has servants, too, to cook and serve his meals, to clean his home, and to be ready to fetch anything he asks for. *(Select child to be a servant. He or she stands behind the rich man)*

This man also has a son. The son knows he will be very rich one day, when the old man dies. *(Select son, who comes to the front)* But this lad is afraid he might be too old to enjoy all that money then; his father is not *so* old, and looks very healthy, and may even live to be ninety! So what does he do? No, he doesn't kill him off — there's an easier way of getting hold of some money to spend. Why not just ask for it? After all, it will be his one day, and he might as well have it now. He could leave home and see the city, perhaps even travel abroad. *(Turn to son)* Ask your father, then, if he'll give it to you now — the amount he'd planned to leave you in his will. *(Child asks — make sure he can be heard)*

What do you think Dad would say? Remember, he loves this boy and wants to see him get on in life. He says yes. *(Turn to father)* Ask the servant to get the money out of the bank. Give it to your son. Wait a minute, though. What do you think your *own* father would say if he was handing over £1,000? He'd probably say, 'Be careful; money doesn't grow on trees, you know. Don't spend it all at once; don't go mad.' This father does the same; he doesn't want the boy to be sorry he's got it.

So, here's the boy, probably still a teenager, with a wallet full of notes. He decides to see the world; he's free, he's got nothing to worry about. Go on, then, son, go and spend it. You could even give some of it away. *(Child proceeds down the side of the hall, pretending to buy on the way, getting rid of his money to those he passes. When he gets to the back of the hall, ask if he has any money left)* Well, if you have, buy some more food and drink, have a party. *(All money should have gone by now)* How are you going to get some more money? Your father? Do you really think you could go back and tell him what a fool you've been? What would he say? 'I told you so,' of course.

What about working for it? But you've ended up in a city that has no jobs to offer, no money for Social Security. Perhaps you had better sell those posh clothes you're wearing. *(Child takes off jacket and/or jersey and shoes and leaves them behind)* And you'd better get out of the city and look for a bit of farm labouring. *(Select a child from the back of the hall to be the farmer)* Here's a farmer: what do you ask him? Luckily, he's just looking for an extra man to look after the animals, especially at feeding time. Give him a bucket of food, farmer, and tell him to get straight out to the pigs. *(Son should go right across the hall at the back)* Well, by now you're tired out. Your feet hurt from all that walking, and you're starving! How about the food in the bucket? Looks and smells revolting, doesn't it, but you haven't a lot of choice.

How long are you going to stand this job? Not long! You could be doing the same sort of thing back home — look how well-fed that servant was! Dressed properly, he was, too. How about going back and asking Dad for a job? Even having to admit you've made a mess of things would be better than this. This is the way back home, so start walking *(Indicate the central passageway)* Slowly, slowly, your feet hurt, and you're very weak.

(Turn to father) Now, Dad, you thought this might happen, didn't you? What are you going to say when you see him coming? 'The young fool, I told him this would happen'? Well, that's what he'd expect. Perhaps you would even refuse to have him home — or at the best make him sleep in the garage or in a barn. He'd have to beg for anything he wants, too. After all, you were right and he was wrong. Here he comes, get ready for it ...

Wait, though. This particular father was better than most, and he did love his son very much. Forget what the boy's done! Go on, welcome him back! You're really pleased to see him. *(Father goes from his position to meet the son coming towards him)* You can put your arm around him and drag him home. He looks awful, doesn't he? Get the servant to fetch some clean clothes. *(Indicate the pile of clothes)* And take the ring off your finger and put it on his; show him you're ready to give him even more than he's already had. Are you happy to be home, son? It was a great welcome, wasn't it?

(Send children to sit down)

89

Prayer
Say or sing the Lord's Prayer.

What were the words at the beginning of that prayer? *Our Father ...* the very best kind of father. Even when we behave just like that son, grabbing what we can, doing stupid things that would be almost unforgivable for a human father, then God, our heavenly Father, welcomes us back without any scolding. We call that 'unconditional love' — no strings attached.

Alternative story: Silver paint
Peter hated it when Mother was in bed. She shouldn't be ill. She should be cooking and washing and cleaning. She should be there to give him a hot drink, or at least a friendly welcome, as he came home from school. Today wouldn't be too bad, though, because he'd bought a new model plane kit with his pocket money and he would be too busy making it up to notice that she wasn't around. First, though, parts of it had to be painted. He couldn't remember where he had last put his paints, and they weren't where he usually kept them.

'Where are my paints?' he stormed in to ask Mother.

'I really haven't seen them, Peter,' Mother said. Her voice wasn't very strong, he noticed, and she was holding her ear as if it was painful. 'Go and look in all your cupboards and drawers.'

Peter stamped into his room. Really, it was too bad. Mother usually knew where everything was. He pulled open every drawer; funny how much rubbish there was, he thought, as he tore at it. No paint, though. What was the good of a lovely plane to make up if he couldn't paint the parts first? Mother must have hidden the paints. Perhaps she'd thrown them away, some of the little tins looked awfully old.

'It's no good!' he shouted as he went into Mother's room again. 'I've just wasted all my money on a model kit that's absolutely no good without paints! You've thrown them away, haven't you?' He bit his lip; it really wasn't the way to talk to Mother at all, especially when she was ill.

'No, Peter, I'm sure I would have noticed,' Mother said wearlily. 'Go and look on top of your wardrobe.'

Peter slammed the door. He climbed on the bed to look on the wardrobe. One small tin of silver paint was there. He'd used it to touch up his bike a month ago. He really needed yellow, but he supposed the silver might do instead. He left the room, trying to ease the lid away from the tin. It was stuck. He felt very cross indeed.

'Rotten thing!' he said, and threw the tin down the stairs. It hit the wall and the lid flew off. Silver paint shot across the wall, splattered the banisters and rolled out in a sticky mess as the tin spun over and over down the stair carpet.

90

Peter stood still, looking at what had happened. Then he rushed to pick up the tin. Soon his hands and his shoes and his school trousers were mottled with silver, too. He cried.

A bedroom door opened and Mother stood there in her nightie. 'Whatever's going on?' she asked.

Peter flung himself at her. 'I didn't mean it to happen, I really didn't,' he sobbed.

Mother didn't say any more. Quietly, she fetched the bottle of turps and two rags. She handed one to Peter, who dabbed at his trousers. Mother was on her hands and knees, rubbing the silver patches on the carpet. Peter wondered how much it hurt her head; she looked very pale.

At last, most of the silver paint had disappeared and Mother had washed Peter's school trousers in the sink. She smiled at him and hugged him. 'All right now?' she asked.

Peter managed a small, sorry smile, and felt a little better. He was glad Mother loved him and had forgiven him. Perhaps he could remember to think how she was feeling before doing a stupid thing like that, next time.

Prayer
Dear Father, help us to remember this story when we go wrong and when we feel we don't know what to do next. We know you are ready to forgive us and welcome us back into your family. Thank you for loving us so much.

Readings
Paul, one of Jesus' early followers, wrote this about love:

I may be able to speak the languages of men and even of angels, but if I have no love, my speech is no more than a noisy gong or a clanging bell. I may have the gift of inspired preaching; I may have all knowledge and understand all secrets; I may have all the faith needed to move mountains — but if I have no love, I am nothing. I may give away everything I have, and even give up my body to be burnt — but if I have no love, this does me no good.

Love is patient and kind; it is not jealous or conceited or proud; love is not ill-mannered or selfish or irritable; love does not keep a record of wrongs; love is not happy with evil, but is happy with the truth. Love never gives up; and its faith, hope, and patience never fail.

(1 Corinthians 13.1-7, GNB)

Here is the story Jesus told about a father's love:

'There was once a man who had two sons; and the younger said to his father, "Father, give me my share of the property." So he divided his estate

91

between them. A few days later the younger son turned the whole of his share into cash and left home for a distant country, where he squandered it in reckless living. He had spent it all, when a severe famine fell upon that country and he began to feel the pinch. So he went and attached himself to one of the local landowners, who sent him on to his farm to mind the pigs. He would have been glad to fill his belly with the pods that the pigs were eating; and no one gave him anything. Then he came to his senses and said, "How many of my father's paid servants have more food than they can eat, and here am I, starving to death! I will set off and go to my father, and say to him, 'Father, I have sinned, against God and against you; I am no longer fit to be called your son; treat me as one of your paid servants.' " So he set out for his father's house. But while he was still a long way off his father saw him, and his heart went out to him. He ran to meet him, flung his arms round him, and kissed him. The father said to his servants, "Quick! fetch a robe, my best one, and put it on him; put a ring on his finger and shoes on his feet. Bring the fatted calf and kill it, and let us have a feast to celebrate the day. For this son of mine was dead and has come back to life; he was lost and is found." And the festivities began.'

(Luke 15.11-20,22-24, NEB)

Hymns
God, my Father, loving me
Sing life, sing love, sing Jesus   (SM 29)
The King of love my shepherd is

Follow-up for the class-room

1   Examine the word *love*. This age-group will probably giggle at the mere mention of the word, connecting it with girl and boy friends, television plays, pop stars; or even at the thought of their parents marrying for love. Most dictionaries define love as 'warm affection'. It would be interesting to examine mother-love; the outward expression of it — kissing, cuddling and hugging; the responsibility of cooking, cleaning and home-making; and also the untiring caring — night vigils, listening to problems, coping with difficult behaviour and emotional anxieties, etc. Encourage discussion about this caring love, and how far it can be seen outside the home: in the school, clubs and community. Draw pictures to show this caring love being expressed.

2   Begin a class scrapbook. Provide newspapers and magazines so that the children can cut out stories and articles of people showing their love for others by caring. The scrapbook could be entitled *Love is real — love is care*.

3   Continue the story of the loving father by talking about the elder brother — did he show real love? In what ways could he have welcomed his brother? What is jealousy? Can it be overcome? (Luke 15.25-32)

Whatever the weather

The Assembly

Talk

Have you ever thought how much the weather governs us and what we do? It is probably the one subject that everybody can talk about. Listen to people as they meet each other, or talk at a bus stop, or on the telephone: 'Good morning, Mrs Brown; lovely weather, isn't it?' or 'Not as warm as yesterday, is it?' or 'Nice to see the rain, the gardens needed it.' or 'Very cold today, isn't it?' The weather is often the first topic of conversation.

We read about it in the papers: 'Heavy rain caused widespread flooding yesterday' or we hear about it on the radio: 'North-easterly gales are approaching Rockall' or we see satellite pictures or diagrammatic forecasts on television.

The weather is important to us. It has a great influence on our lives. It can cause us to do all sorts of things: if it rains we hurry for shelter, or put up an umbrella, or put on a mackintosh. If a strong wind blows we struggle to walk against it, or get blown along by it. When the sun shines warmly we take off our clothes! You wouldn't wear two jumpers and a thick overcoat in a heatwave! In this country we have a great variety of weather. How dull it would be if we knew that from July 1 each year we were certain to get a month of cold, wet weather; or from April 15 we would have six weeks of sunshine, so hot that all the rivers dried up and the crops died.

In the weather which God gives us, in this country, he gives us *hope*, and something we could call *expectancy*. It may be raining today, but we always have hope that it will be sunny later on — today or tomorrow or next week. It may be scorching hot, but we hope that before too long the rain will come to cool us down and feed the earth. We may have dull, cold days, but we can hope that there will be a fall of snow before the winter is over.

We all need *hope*. It is *looking forward*, just as you look forward to your birthday, or to the summer holiday, or to Christmas. When Paul was writing to Christians living in great danger in Rome, he used these words:

And may the God of hope fill you with all joy and peace by your faith in him, until, by the power of the Holy Spirit, you overflow with hope. *(Romans 15.13, NEB)*

94

Alternative talk
Use the dramatisation given below or, if this is not possible, read it through,
or read the biblical account in Acts 27, and tell it as a straightforward narrative.

Preparation
Copies of the dramatisation will be needed for those taking part — the
Narrator, Luke and Paul. It should be rehearsed before the Assembly. Storm
music could be played on a record or tape, or by a percussion group.

Dramatisation
Leader: St Paul was a great worker for Christ, but life was never easy for him.
Listen to this account of a time when he was caught in a terrible storm at sea.
Narrator: Paul had been tried by the Roman Governor in Palestine for being a
dangerous nuisance, and it was decided that he should be sent to the Roman
Emperor in Italy.
Luke: When it was decided that we should sail to Italy, they handed Paul and
some other prisoners over to Julius, an officer in the Roman army. Julius was
a just man, and kind to Paul.
Paul: The winds were blowing against us, so we sailed on the sheltered side of
the island of Cyprus until we came to a place called Myra, in Lycia. There a
ship was found sailing for Italy, so we prisoners were put on board.
Luke: We sailed slowly because of the direction of the wind, and kept close to
the coast of Crete on the way. At last we came to a place called 'Safe Harbours'
— but we stayed there too long. The bad weather of October had just begun.
Paul gave the men on board this advice:
Paul: Men, I see that from now on our voyage will be dangerous; the ship will
probably be damaged, and men's lives could be lost.
Luke: But the captain pointed out that the harbour was not a good one in which
to stay for the winter, and most of the sailors were in favour of putting out to
sea. There was a fair possibility that we could reach Phoenix, further round
the coast, and spend the winter there.
Narrator: A soft wind from the south began to blow, so the anchor was raised
and the ship began to sail as close as possible along the coast of Crete.
Luke: But soon the wind changed, and a strong north-easterly began to blow.
The sailors had to give up trying to steer the ship, and had to let her be carried
along in the wind. The next day the storm was still bad, so some of the ship's
cargo, and then some of her equipment, was thrown overboard to lighten
her. For many days we couldn't see the sun — or the stars — and the wind was
violent. We gave up hope of being saved. By this time most of the men were
desperately tired, and many were hungry because they had not eaten for
days. Paul decided to talk to them:
Paul: You should have listened to me earlier, and we might have avoided all
this damage and loss. But don't lose heart: every man will be saved, even if we

95

lose the ship. I'm sure God wants me to face the Emperor in Rome, and he will help you to survive as well.

Luke: For a fortnight we were tossed about in the storm. Then one night — about midnight — something told the sailors that we were near land, so they tested the sea's depth at intervals, and found that it was getting shallower. They were afraid we would hit rocks, though, so they lowered four great anchors from the back of the ship to try to stop her drifting in the darkness. Then they sat back and prayed for daylight.

Paul: Some of them panicked and tried to get off the ship in a small boat, but I told them to stay where they were if they wanted to be saved. Just before dawn I begged them to eat some food; they would need all their strength if they were to survive.

Luke: There, in the middle of the storm, with the ship tossing and rolling, Paul took bread and gave thanks, just as Jesus did at the last supper, and ate it. The sailors seemed to regain some courage when they saw this, and ate some food. Later they lightened the ship by throwing all the extra cargo of wheat overboard.

Paul: At daylight we could see a coastline. No one seemed to know where we were, but we could see a bay with a beach, and the sailors decided to try to run the ship aground there.

Luke: The sail was raised, and the anchors cut loose, and to our relief the ship was driven by the wind towards the shore. Suddenly we hit a sandbank with a loud grating crash, and stuck fast. The stern was quickly broken up by the terrific waves. We all became very frightened, and the soldiers wanted to kill the prisoners there and then, so that they couldn't swim ashore and escape. Luckily, the officer in charge stopped them doing this; I think he was anxious to save Paul.

Paul: The officer ordered those who could swim to jump overboard and get to the shore. The rest were to follow, clutching any drifting wood they could find.

Narrator: And so everyone survived. They had been shipwrecked on the island of Malta. They were looked after for the rest of the winter by the inhabitants there. Three months later they set sail again for Italy, and when they arrived Paul was taken to Rome.

Readings

Sometimes, especially in stormy weather, people become frightened. This happened once to Jesus' friends:

Jesus said to his disciples, 'Let us go across to the other side of the lake.' So they left the crowd; the disciples got into the boat in which Jesus was already sitting, and they took him with them. Other boats were there too. Suddenly a strong wind blew up, and the waves began to spill over into the boat, so that it was about to fill with water. Jesus was in the back of the boat, sleeping with his head on a pillow. The disciples woke him up and said, 'Teacher, don't you care that we are about to die?'

Jesus stood up and commanded the wind, 'Be quiet!' and he said to the waves, 'Be still!' The wind died down, and there was a great calm.

(Mark 4.35-39, GNB)

Long before the time of Jesus, the ancient Hebrews believed that God could make the storm quiet again, too. This reading is from one of the psalms:

Others there are who go to sea in ships
and make their living on the wide waters.
These men have seen the acts of the Lord
and his marvellous doings in the deep.
At his command the storm-wind rose
and lifted the waves high.
Carried up to heaven, plunged down to the depths,
tossed to and fro in peril,
they reeled and staggered like drunken men,
and their seamanship was all in vain.
So they cried to the Lord in their trouble,
and he brought them out of their distress.
The storm sank to a murmur
and the waves of the sea were stilled.

(Psalm 107.23-29, NEB)

Prayer .
On windy days, remember those in danger at sea, who might be frightened by the weather: fishermen, rescue patrols, men on oil rigs, divers and explorers. Let us pray that God will be with them:

O God, giver of the weather, help us to love its changes and to be grateful for the feeling of hope it can give us. Be with any who are made afraid by the weather, on land or sea or in the air; give them courage, give them hope, and give them a quiet certainty that you are with them at all times.

Hymns
Eternal Father, strong to save
He's got the whole world in his hands   (CP 19)

Music
Mendelssohn: Overture The Hebrides (Fingal's Cave).

Follow-up for the class-room

1   Read again the story of the storm on Galilee (Mark 4.36-39), letting the children make the storm sounds. Paint or draw pictures of the story, trying to get the storm atmosphere.

2   Make a wind-vane for use outside. (Many books give simple instructions for these.) Keep a wind-chart, showing wind direction, every day for a month. Find out by means of the chart, and a daily note of general weather conditions, if there seems to be any connection between them.

3   In small groups, which could report back to the rest of the class, find out about some of the following: weather satellites, radar, rain gauges, barometers, anemometers, etc.

4   Read with the children Matthew 7.24-27, about the two house builders, and dramatise or illustrate.

The Name of God

It is suggested that the two Assemblies included under this heading are taken consecutively. The purpose of the first Assembly is to help the children to understand and appreciate the faiths of people who are not Christians, especially children with whom they work at school.

The Assembly (1)

Story
The new girl's name was Ghania. Two months earlier she had been living in Pakistan, where it was hot and dry at this time of the year. In Britain it was almost winter, and the weather was getting steadily colder. Ghania arrived at school in a thin cotton dress and a cardigan; Karen felt sorry for her, but was glad to see she wore a warm pair of brown tights. Ghania was very shy and quiet, and every day she joined a special class for an hour to help her learn more English.

It was Karen's job to look after the new girl. 'Make sure she knows what to do,' Miss James had said, 'especially at break and lunch time.'

In the playground Karen asked Ghania to join the game she was playing with some friends. Ghania didn't say much, but seemed to prefer to watch. At lunch time she queued with Karen for her plate of food but would only accept the potatoes and carrots from the dinner lady.

'Don't you like sausages?' asked Karen.

'I don't know,' said Ghania, and they hardly spoke again until after the bell went for afternoon lessons.

In class the next day they had the story of Moses. Karen noticed that Ghania seemed to know about him, which surprised her.

'Do you believe in God?' she asked Ghania, in a whisper.

'Of course,' said Ghania. 'We called him Allah.'

'Do you say prayers?' Karen asked.

'We say prayers five times a day,' said Ghania.

'Five times a day?' Karen asked, her voice no longer a whisper.

Miss James had heard the last remark, and stopped talking about Moses

99

and the burning bush he found in the desert. She looked at Karen with a question in her eyes.

'Ghania knows about Moses, Miss James,' Karen said. 'She believes in God, too, and she prays five times a day!'

'But I'm not a Christian,' Ghania said firmly.

'Ghania is a Muslim,' explained Miss James to the class. 'You call God "Allah", don't you?' she asked.

'Yes,' said Ghania. 'And we are taught that Moses was one of his prophets.'

'What about Jesus?' asked Karen.

'We believe he was also a great prophet,' said Ghania. 'But the greatest prophet was Mohammed, peace be upon him.'

Karen had never heard of Mohammed. 'Do you read the Bible?' she asked.

Ghania shook her head. 'The Bible is the Christians' holy book,' she said. 'Muslims read the Koran. It contains the word of God as given to Mohammed, peace be upon him.'

'How else are Muslims different from Christians?' Miss James asked her. 'We'd like to understand what it means to be a Muslim.'

'We only eat meat from animals killed in a special way, and we never eat any meat from pigs. That's why I only eat vegetable dishes at school,' replied Ghania. 'And Muslim girls must always keep their arms and legs covered, especially after they are eleven or twelve years old. At home we wash carefully five times a day before we say our prayers to Allah. And we always kneel with our faces towards our holy city, Mecca, which is in Saudi Arabia. Sometimes we fast — go without food and drink — all day, although we can eat after sunset.'

'How hungry and thirsty she must get,' thought Karen, but admired her for the self-discipline she needed.

Ghania *was* different, but Karen felt she was beginning to understand her.

'Praise be to God,' said Miss James, just before they all went home that day.

Karen smiled at Ghania.

'Allahu Akbar — God is the greatest,' said Ghania, and Karen knew she had made a good friend.

Prayers
Almighty, powerful God, Father of all, we meet hand in hand with people of other faiths. Join us together in love and understanding, so that we may live and work together in peace.

A prayer of Mohammed
O Lord, grant us to love you:
grant that we may love those that love you;
grant that we may do the deeds that win your love.

Whatever we believe, and however we worship, let us each turn to the people on either side of us and say the word 'Peace'.

Hymns
I belong to a family, the biggest on earth   (CP 69, SM 7)
In Christ there is no east or west
Now thank we all our God

Readings
Listen to the opening verses of one of the great songs of the Bible, which praises the name of God:

I will always thank the Lord;
   I will never stop praising him.
I will praise him for what he has done;
   may all who are oppressed listen and be glad!
Proclaim with me the Lord's greatness;
   let us praise his name together!

(Psalm 34.1-3, GNB)

The Bible has a story of how God spoke to Moses:

   The Lord came down in a cloud, stood with him there, and pronounced his holy name, the Lord. The Lord then passed in front of him and called out, 'I, the Lord, am a God who is full of compassion and pity, who is not easily angered and who shows great love and faithfulness.'

(Exodus 34.5-6, GNB)

Paul wrote these words in a letter to Timothy, a young assistant missionary:

   Continue in the truths that you were taught and firmly believe. You know who your teachers were, and you remember that ever since you were a child, you have known the Holy Scriptures, which are able to give you the wisdom that leads to salvation through faith in Christ Jesus. All Scripture is inspired by God and is useful for teaching the truth, rebuking error, correcting faults, and giving instruction for right living, so that the person who serves God may be fully qualified and equipped to do every kind of good deed.

(2 Timothy 3.14-17, GNB)

Follow-up for the class-room

1   If you have children of other faiths in your class, do your best to see that they are included here. Ask them to obtain permission from home to attend, if they are normally excluded from RE lessons. Let there be a general discussion, with questions and answers, between all the children, so that they can find out more about other religions, their scriptures, festivals and customs. The 'Our Friends' series published by NCEC gives information about other faiths and cultural backgrounds. These books are written for the 8-12 age group, but teachers will find them useful. The six titles are 'Our Muslim Friends', 'Our Christian Friends', 'Our Hindu Friends', 'Our Jewish Friends', 'Our Sikh Friends', and 'Our Buddhist Friends'.

2   If all the children in the class come from Christian backgrounds, try to encourage a discussion about different denominations, and discover how worship and private devotions may differ one from another.

3   Make a large wall picture showing children from many countries and faiths joining hands, either in a long line, or round a 'globe'. Add the Hindu prayer, 'O God, let there be peace, peace, peace'.

4   Collect sayings from the major scriptural writings, eg:
Ōm. Let us meditate on the glorious light of the Creator. (Hindu, from the Vedas)   *Prayer is better then sleep!* (Muslim, from the Koran)   *Love the Lord your God with all your heart and soul and strength.*(Jewish, from the Torah)   *Should any man smite thee, return not blow for blow, nay, kiss his feet that smiteth thee and go peacefully homeward.* (Sikh, from the Guru Granth Sahib)   *Love one another, just as I love you.* (Christian, from the Bible)
   These could be written out and decorated, to make a frieze, or made into small, individual books.

The Assembly (2)

Story: Moses meets God
It was difficult to find much grass for the flocks of sheep and goats to eat. Moses looked across the wild land, brown and dry, and shielded his eyes against the sun. The sheep jostled each other as they mouthed at the dry tufts of the desert grasses, and the goats climbed the higher rocks in search of food.
   Moses knew there might be better pasture further up the side of the

mountain in front of him. Calling the sheep and goats, he rallied them into a straggling line, and led them higher up the slope.

It was hot and dusty, and Moses rubbed his hands across his eyes. He thought he could see flames ahead, but perhaps it was only some kind of illusion created by the blazing sun. As he got nearer he was sure that a bush must have caught fire: it seemed to be alight, but somehow it was not being destroyed.

'How strange,' he thought. 'It seems to be burning, yet it isn't. The twigs are still whole and strong. If it was on fire the whole bush would be burnt to ashes by now.' He just had to get closer to see what was happening.

Suddenly he heard a voice. Could it be coming from the bush? Someone must be up here with him on these lonely hills! And whoever it was must know him, because he kept hearing his own name — 'Moses! Moses!'

'Yes,' he said. 'I'm here!'

He still couldn't see anybody, and the bush was still bright and glowing. 'Stop!' said the voice, as Moses edged nearer. 'Don't come any closer. Take off your sandals, because you are standing on holy ground.'

Moses stopped and slid off his loose shoes. The dry earth and the stones felt hot to his bare feet, and the air shimmered in a misty haze. He lifted his head to look at the bush.

'I am the God of your ancestors, the God of Abraham, Isaac and Jacob,' said the same mysterious voice, and Moses knew that he was meeting the great, almighty God that his people had always worshipped. He put his arm over his eyes — he could not look at God; it was fearful and wonderful enough that he could hear his voice.

'I am sending you, Moses, to lead the people — your people — out of Egypt,' the voice of God went on. 'I have seen them suffer, and they must be saved.'

'Me?' asked Moses. 'Why me? I'm nobody! How can I go to the king and ask him to let the slaves go? And the slaves themselves will ask, "Who sent you?" What do I tell them? What do I call you?'

'I am who I am,' God replied. 'Tell the people that the One who is called "I am" has sent you to them.'

When Moses had listened to all the things God was asking him to do, he was very frightened. 'No, Lord, please send someone else,' he pleaded. He knew he had never been a very good speaker, and he wasn't likely to have become one in the last hour or so!

'You shall have someone to help you,' God replied. 'Tell your brother, Aaron, what I have told you, and he can speak for you. But I will be with you, and will tell you what to say.'

Later, the people of Israel, in slavery in Egypt, learnt from Moses and Aaron what had happened on the mountain that day, and as they were led out of Egypt by Moses they praised the name of the God who had delivered them.

(From Exodus 3.1-17)

Prayer

O God, almighty God, you who were before the beginning of time itself; you who saw all things created; you who saw all earth formed, and all history lived: we worship you. Help us to see you, as Moses did, in our daily lives. As we work and play, keep us ready to listen to you, and willing to answer.

Hymns

The God of Abraham praise
The God of love my shepherd is
The Lord's my shepherd

Reading

Moses must have felt that God was guiding him, as a shepherd guides and leads his sheep, especially when he began the long and difficult journey back towards the land God had promised to the Israelite people. Much later, a song was sung by the people; it talks of God the shepherd:

God is my shepherd!

I shall lack nothing —
    he lets me lie down on green grass,
leads me by quiet streams,
    makes me a new man.
He guides me along the right tracks,
    because he is what he is;
when I go through the pitch-black gorge,
    nothing frightens me!

You are with me,
    club and staff at the ready —
        making me strong!

You are my host, I am your guest
    while enemies look helplessly on!
You bathe my head with oil,
    fill my cup to the brim!

Your goodness and love shall follow me
    all my days!
God's home is my home
    for ever!

(Psalm 23, WQ)

Follow-up for the class-room

1 Let the children use their Bibles to find other names by which God was known in biblical times, eg Jehovah or Yahweh (Exodus 6.3, NEB), Holy One (Isaiah 10.20, NEB), Lord of lords and King of kings (1 Timothy 6.15, NEB), Father (Mark 14.36, NEB), etc.

2 Write as many prayer 'openings' as possible; this will give the teacher some insight as to how the children have come to know, and think of, God. Write a prayer of worship, such as Moses might have prayed after his encounter with God.

3 Illustrate or dramatise the story of the burning bush: Exodus 3.1-17.

Whitsun — birthday of the Church

An assembly taken near to Whit Sunday can be used to remind the children why this is such an important day for the Christian Church. It is a day which should be as festive and exciting as Christmas, and as awe-inspiring and uplifting as Easter, and yet a great many pupils in our schools will have no idea of its significance.

The Assembly

Preparation
A hand-held hair drier and a bunch of streamers will be needed.

Demonstration and talk
Invite a child to assist, and ask him or her to hold up the streamers, which should hang downwards limply. Then switch on the hair drier and show how the current of air from it makes the streamers flow as though they were being blown by a strong wind. Ask if the children are reminded of a windy day, when the power of the wind can be seen as it blows papers about, or blows a line of washing, or blows off hats!

The disciples of Jesus knew a good deal about the power of the wind and of water, especially the fishermen Peter and Andrew, James and John. They had felt the powerful currents beneath the waves, and had made use of the wind to catch the sails of their boats. They knew just how to adjust the ropes to pull the sails one way or the other so that the wind would drive the boats into the centre of the lake; and there they could lower the sail so that they drifted slowly, looking for the shoals of fish. They had gazed down into the deep water, and knew how it could change from a smooth glass-like pool into a heaving mass of dangerous waves. Sometimes they had to drag and pull at the ropes, trying to get the wind to work for them so that they could reach the safety of land before they were swept into the sea. They had learnt to watch the clouds and to test the wind's direction, so that they could prepare for the weather. Even then, the winds could come suddenly, rushing down through the hills by the lakeside, and catch them unawares. Yes, the wind had power; the wind *was* power. It was something that they could not control; something much stronger than they were.

After Jesus died, the disciples remembered that he had promised them power. They wondered how it would be given to them. They certainly needed strength and courage to do the job of work Jesus expected them to carry on for him. They believed they had seen him for the lat time, when he had told them to wait in Jerusalem. Now another Jewish feast was near, a holy day called Pentecost. Everybody was in the streets, beginning the celebrations. The friends of Jesus — many more than those first few disciples — met again, secretly, in a room in the city.

Suddenly they heard a noise. It grew stronger and louder, a sound like a rushing wind. They thought of the powerful wind of Galilee. Whatever was happening? It grew louder and louder, filling the whole house. Then suddenly it died down, and they realised what had happened: the gift promised by Jesus had come, the gift of power. They were no longer afraid and helpless, they had the whole world to conquer – and conquer it they would!

They flung open the window shutters and shouted from the open doorway, and spilled down into the street. They found they could speak words they hardly knew the meaning of, words that could be understood even by the foreigners in the street outside. What a meeting it was! Power had been given to them; power that, like the wind, they had no control over, that was stronger than they were; power to speak for Jesus; power to carry on his work.

And so at Pentecost, in Jerusalem, the church was born — the Christian Church, starting with a small band of Christ's followers. Just as at Christmas we celebrate Christ's birth, so at Whitsun, or Pentecost, we celebrate the birth of his Church.

Alternative story: The lights
Clare was excited because she was going out long after it was dark, and she wasn't often allowed to do that. She had had her tea, and watched some television, and at last it was time to go.

'Come on, jump in the car,' shouted Dad.

Clare hurried into her warm coat and wrapped a scarf round her neck. Half an hour's drive and they would be there — at the sea-side, on a cold autumn evening.

When they arrived the place was crowded with people gathered along the sea front. Some looked out at the black waves, some walked on the pier in the dark, and others peered into the shop windows.

Clare looked at Dad's watch — it was almost time. Soon it would all look so different. The crowds were ready, too, and people stopped chattering and everyone looked up in readiness. Then, suddenly, the power was switched on, and there were lights — hundreds of dancing, coloured light-bulbs: patterns, and pictures, and funny cartoon animals, all formed in lights. It was like fairyland, or a magician's grotto. It was beautiful.

Nearly two thousand years ago, the friends of Jesus waited, knowing that something was going to happen, but not sure what it would be like. Then a power was suddenly 'switched on' by God, and invisible lights in all the followers of Jesus began to shine. It was as if the watching people could see them glow as they began to talk, without fear, and in the open, about this man Jesus.

On Whit Sunday, Christian Churches all over the world remember this 'switch on', the birthday celebration of power that began so long ago.

Poem
Rush of the wild wind,
Indoors not out;
Lifting our heads high,
Lifting our hearts,
It came as a sigh,
It grew to a shout,
Wind come from heaven
To fold us about.

Release from our chains,
Hope for our fear,
Giving our lips song
Right from our hearts.
It cannot be wrong
For others to hear;
Wind come from heaven —
For ever be near.

Readings
Here is the story of the first Whit Sunday:

For forty days after his death he (Jesus) appeared to them many times in ways that proved beyond doubt that he was alive. They saw him, and he talked with them about the Kingdom of God. And when they came together, he gave them this order: 'Do not leave Jerusalem, but wait for the gift I told you about, the gift my Father promised.'

When the day of Pentecost came, all the believers were gathered together in one place. Suddenly there was a noise from the sky which sounded like a strong wind blowing, and it filled the whole house where they were sitting. Then they saw what looked like tongues of fire which spread out and touched each person there. They were all filled with the Holy Spirit and began to talk in other languages, as the Spirit enabled them to speak.

(Acts 1.3-4; 2.1-4, GNB)

As the disciples realised that they had received the power that had been promised them, they became more adventurous for Christ. This story tells how Peter and John used their power:

One day Peter and John went to the Temple at three o'clock in the afternoon, the hour for prayer. There at the Beautiful Gate, as it was called, was a man who had been lame all his life. Every day he was carried to the gate to beg for money from the people who were going into the Temple. When he saw Peter and John going in, he begged them to give him something. They looked straight at him, and Peter said, 'Look at us!' So he looked at them, expecting to get something from them. But Peter said to him, 'I have no money at all, but I give you what I have: in the name of Jesus Christ of Nazareth I order you to get up and walk!' Then he took him by his right hand and helped him up. At once the man's feet and ankles became strong; he jumped up, stood on his feet, and started walking around. Then he went into the Temple with them, walking and jumping and praising God.

(Acts 3.1-8, GNB)

Later, Peter was taken to court for creating a disturbance. When he was questioned, he said, 'We cannot stop speaking of what we ourselves have seen and heard.'

Prayer
Give us strength, too, O God, so that, like Peter, we cannot be stopped from telling what is right and good. We are happy about the birthday of your Church; help us to tell everyone about it. Peter was laughed at, and jeered at, and told to be quiet, but he had the power of God in him. May we be like Peter, and go on praising you, even in difficult times.

Hymns
Give me joy in my heart, keep me praising
Holy Spirit, hear us
Spirit of God, as strong as the wind   (CP 63)

Music
Mendelssohn: Symphony No 4 (The Italian) — Finale.

Follow-up for the class-room

1   Organise a mini-party in the class-room. Plan ahead with the children how best to celebrate the Church's birthday, and hold the 'feast' as near to Whit Sunday as possible. Include a few games, biscuits and orangeade, singing of joyful songs, eg 'He's got the whole world in his hands', 'Go, tell it on the mountain'. Sing 'Happy Birthday', adjusting the words to the occasion. Remind the children of the reason for the celebration.

2   Plan a present for a local church, eg a class-made decoration such as a stained-glass window design; or a large birthday card, designed, executed and signed by the whole class.

3   With older pupils, read and dramatise the trial of Peter and John after the Gate Beautiful healing incident: Acts 3.1-10; 4.1-23.

4   Seeing the light: examine how night-time became more bearable with the growth of lighting aids, from burning torches to electricity. Link with suddenly seeing the solution to a problem, as the disciples must have felt at Whitsun; or the more powerful the light the further it will penetrate, as the power the disciples received was so strong that it has shone across thousands of miles, and hundreds of years, since that first Pentecostal happening.

Signs and Symbols

The Assembly

Poem
Here is silence;
our voices still,
imprisoned in the castle of our souls.
Silence of many, silence of all;
rising, surrounding,
enclosing.
Silence so rich
that even our thoughts are lost in it.
Silence of lips,
silence of bodies,
making us one;
wrapping us round; bound;
silent unity; giving us
a oneness with the moment,
lifting us away from time.
Here is silence.

Talk
Pretend, for a few moments, that your voices have died: everyone is
completely dumb. Remember this while I ask you some questions, which
you must answer.

This is (Friday) morning (afternoon); am I right? You have replied — by
nodding your heads.

There are only four people in this room; am I right? You have replied
again, by shaking your heads.

Now another question: What is the Russian translation of 'Will you play
with me?' You have answered again — I saw you. Some of you raised your
eyebrows, some tilted your heads, some of you opened your mouths· in
astonishment. All those signs told me the answer, and the answer was that
you don't know!

(Ask the next question of one child by name) How would you tell that a boy in the row in front of you is nuts — crackers — barmy? You mustn't speak, remember, just show me. *(Child will probably touch his head with his finger)* Good.

(Ask another child) How would you tell me that the ice cream you are eating is absolutely gorgeous — fabulous? *(Child will probably rub his stomach, lick his lips, smile, or he might make a forefinger touching thumb-tip gesture)* Right. ·

Just see how you have been able to communicate without actually speaking! *(Show again the finger to thumb gesture that could have been used in answer to the last question)* Most people in this country know that this signal means 'great!' But, if you were in Japan, it would mean something else: it would indicate money. If you were in France, and you made the sign but frowned at the same time, it would mean that something was absolutely worthless. We all make signs, but they may vary from country to country.

Gangs sometimes have secret signals — a secret way of shaking hands, perhaps, or a sign drawn with the fingers on another member's palm. These signs are made so that one member may recognise another.

It was like that very early on, when being a Christian was like being a member of a secret society. In the days after Jesus' death it was very dangerous to go round broadcasting the fact that you were one of his followers, but there were plenty of secret meetings, if only you could find out about them from another Christian. So how could you tell if another man or woman was a Christian? Suppose you were standing in the market place when another person came along and stood beside you; Christians weren't dressed differently, and they didn't speak with a certain kind of accent, so what was the secret sign? You just picked up a stick or a stone, and scratched the ground or the wall with it, making a picture of a fish as you did so. If the other person was not a Christian, it would mean nothing. If he was a follower of Christ, then his eyes would light up at the signal, and you could begin to whisper together about your faith.

Today, real Christians are still difficult to identify. Some of them, like ministers or vicars, often wear a special collar, a white, 'back-to-front one', that tells you what they do. It is easy to see that they belong to a Christian church. But ordinary people also have signs that they are Christians: if they — and that means you, too — always wear happy smiles and have friendly, helpful hands, these can be the signs that other Christian people will recognise.

Readings
When you are older you will often hear Christians speaking about their 'faith'. This means their belief in Jesus Christ. Just as members of other societies need signs and rules, so do followers of Jesus. These words were

written by a man called James; they are in a collection of instructions for Christians included in the Bible:

My brothers, what good is it for someone to say that he has faith if his actions do not prove it? Can that faith save him? Suppose there are brothers or sisters who need clothes and don't have enough to eat. What good is there in your saying to them, 'God bless you! Keep warm and eat well!' — if you don't give them the necessities of life? So it is with faith: if it is alone and includes no actions, then it is dead.

But someone will say, 'One person has faith, another has actions.' My answer is, 'Show me how anyone can have faith without actions. I will show you my faith by my actions.'

(James 2.14-18, GNB)

Paul wrote:

We who are the friends of Jesus are, as I have already said, like a human body with its different parts. We are many persons, but we are one 'body'. Each of us is like a different part of the body, and we are here to help one another, as the different parts of the body help one another.

Each of us has different gifts; God has seen to that. We must use them. For example: some of us are able to understand God's Way more clearly than others; some of us deal with business better; some of us are teachers; some of us are speakers. Let us use our different gifts with God's help. And so with everything we do. If we give, let us be generous givers; if we are leaders, let us be energetic leaders; if we are helping others, let us be cheerful helpers.

(Romans 12.4-8, NW)

Prayer
Lord Jesus Christ, help us to show by our faces that we love you, by our hands that we serve you, and by our voices that we follow you. May all our actions be Christ-like, so that we shall be recognised as members of your Christian family.

Hymns
A little child may know
One man's hands can't break a prison down   (SM 21)
Stand up, stand up for Jesus

Follow-up for the class-room

1   Learn more about signs and signals. From library books begin to build a project using pictures as a means of communication: cave paintings, picture writing, tracking signs, map signs, etc.

2   Go into more detail about why a fish was used as a Christian symbol. The Greek word for fish was ICHTHUS. I stood for IESOUS — Jesus; CH for CHRISTOS — Christ; TH for THEOU — of God; U for UIOS — Son; S for SOTER — Saviour. Put together, the fish stood for 'Jesus Christ, God's Son, Saviour'. Make a wall chart bearing the fish sign and an explanation.

3   Look at other Christian symbols. IHS: this came from the first three letters of the Greek form of the word IESOUS (Jesus). Some believe it came from the Latin words JESUS HOMINUM SALVATOR which means 'Saviour of Men'. Look at the symbol of the cross, the cock on the weather-vane over a church, the lamb, the anchor, hot-cross buns, Chi Rho ☧ etc.

4   Examine more hand-signals: those used for traffic, or by firemen, or by ground-staff at airports, etc, down to simple ones that are used every day, for waving, beckoning, answering questions, pointing.

5   Find out about the symbolism and signals of flags: semaphore, nautical messages; visual representations of countries, eg Japan, Canada, Israel; flags of organisations, eg United Nations, Olympic Games, Red Cross.

Additional story: The flag he loved
Flags are flown everywhere, all over the world. There is even one on the moon, put there by the astronauts. Flags are signs: they give us information about people, such as the queen, or about countries. Our Union Jack is recognised everywhere as being the symbol of the British people. Flags tell us, too, about organisations: there is a flag for the Red Cross, for Scouts, for Guides, for other youth organisations, and there is even a flag for the Olympic Games.
    This is a true story about someone who loved the Union Jack and all that it stood for.

    Alfred Sadd had travelled from his home in Essex half way across the world to the Gilbert Islands. He was only twenty-three, and had recently become a minister. He was now proud to be called the Revd Alfred Sadd. He had

114

always been one for adventure, so he had asked the London Missionary Society in London to send him abroad as a missionary. The Gilbert Islands had plenty of adventure to offer: a group of small islands in the middle of the Pacific Ocean, right on the line of the equator — the hottest part of the earth. In those days, before the Second World War, they were largely inhabited by wild, excitable natives who, living in their jungle homes, did not often see white men. Alfred worked in a little Christian church there, and soon many of the black people were his friends.

A few years later, in 1942, the Gilbert Islands were invaded by the Japanese. Most of the Europeans who lived and worked on the islands left hurriedly, but Alfred Sadd stayed on. He had spent the last few years building up a strong church of Christians, and he could not desert them now. For two years, Alfred's relatives at home, and the Missionary Society for which he worked, could get no news of him, and were terribly worried.

At last the Japanese were thrown out of the little islands, but by then the Revd Alfred Sadd was dead. One of his native friends sent a letter to the Missionary Society which told the people of Britain what had happened to him.

Any white people left on the islands, the letter said, had been lined up by Japanese troops. Alfred Sadd was one of those people; most of the others were soldiers from New Zealand. A Union Jack was laid on the ground in front of them, and Alfred was ordered to walk over it. To Alfred this was as good as asking him to betray his country. 'Never!' he thought, and he walked up to the flag, but then turned right to avoid stepping on it. The Japanese were angry, and he was ordered back again. This time he turned to the left when he reached the flag.

'Go back again!' barked the Japanese commander, seething with rage. Again Alfred walked up to the flag. Disobedience this time would mean death, he knew. As his feet reached the flag he made a quick decision. Bending down, he gathered the Union Jack in his arms and kissed it. This time there were no more chances. With the other young men, Alfred was marched off to be shot. He saw the faces of the men with him, frightened and miserable, and he joked with them, trying to cheer them up.

They were lined up with Alfred in the centre of the line. He stepped forward for a moment and turned to give a few words of cheer and strength to the row of men. Then he stepped back to join them, but made sure that he was a little in front of them. When the sound of gunfire rang out, Alfred was the first to fall and die.

His native friends, secretly watching in terrible fear, knew that Alfred Sadd had not only told them about Jesus Christ: he had lived a Christian life, and he had died bravely. They erected a wooden cross — the sign of Christ — so that he would be remembered in the Gilbert Islands for years to come.

Speaking to God

The Assembly

Preparation
You will need to set up, talk over, and possibly rehearse, the three short scenes.
Props needed: a toy telephone and a screen; a toy-box and an old toy car.
   Alternatively, the action of the scenes could be told in story form, with the talk following the story.

Drama
Scene 1   A child is seen telephoning a shop; have the person 'answering' hidden behind screen, so that he can be heard but not seen.
Child: Hello, Makesure Supermarket? My mother's ill, and she wants some things sent up today.
Answerer: Makesure Supermarket. You are speaking to Makesure Supermarket.
Child: Good. Could you ...
Answerer: This is an automatic answering service. Please state your name and address, and then give your order as clearly as possible.
Child: Oh dear ... *(Looks at phone in bewilderment, then puts receiver down)*

Scene 2   Teacher, acting as mother, with a small child, who must give the impression of being about three or four years old.
Child: Mum! Mum! Can I have a bicycle?
Mother: When you're older, perhaps. We'll see.
Child: Mum, can I have a blue tomato for dinner?
Mother: A blue tomato! Of course not — we've only got red ones!
Child: Mum, can I borrow Daddy's razor? I want to shave.
Mother: No, you can't! That would be far too dangerous!
Child: Mum, can I have a drink of water?
Mother: Climb on that chair, then you will be able to help yourself.

Scene 3   Teacher, acting as mother, with a boy and girl.
Mother: Go and choose a toy to take to the toy service at school. Remember lots

116

of children have no toys to play with, and many of them wouldn't have presents at Christmas if it wasn't for toy services like yours.

Boy (looking in box): Here's an old car. It's got two wheels missing. I don't want that old thing. That will do!

Girl: I don't want to give any of my toys away. I want them all!

(Children return to mother)

Mother (looking at boy's toy): Oh, that isn't very kind. How could anyone play with that?

Girl (smugly): I knew you were being unkind!

Mother: What about you? Where's the toy you're going to give?

Girl: I'm not giving anything broken, like he is. I'm just not giving anything.

Mother: You're both as bad as each other.

(Pause)

Boy: Yes, we're both wrong. I'm sorry.

Girl: So am I. Let's go and find something really good.

Talk

We've seen three very short plays. Let's look at what was happening in each of them.

In the first one a child was trying to get in touch with a shop. She thought it was going to be easy, but when she came to do it, she found there was a sort of barrier. She found herself talking to a machine.

Let's pretend she was trying to get in touch with God — that she was praying. It would be awful to come up against that sort of barrier. But to talk to God we don't need to go through a machine — we may be sure God doesn't have some kind of automatic answering service! He can be spoken to at any time, and anywhere, and he is ready to listen. He knows each of us personally, and is waiting for us to call him.

In the second play a mother was being pestered by her small child, and each time he asked a question, the mother was patient enough to listen, and to reply. First, the child asked for a bicycle. Mother knew he wasn't big enough for one, and she told him he must wait. Sometimes we may ask God for things in our prayers, and when they are not given to us we often think, 'God isn't there. He didn't answer'. But perhaps the answer is simply that we must wait.

Then the child asked his mother for a blue tomato! Whoever heard of a blue tomato? Sometimes we ask God, in our prayers, for impossible things.

Then he asked if he could have a razor. She said 'No!' very definitely, because it would have been dangerous to have said 'Yes'. Sometimes we ask God for things which would eventually do us harm, and God is just as likely (as that mother was) to say 'No'.

117

Lastly, the child asked his mother for a drink of water. She could have stopped what she was doing, filled a cup with water, and given it to him. But she told him to do it himself, and showed him how to start. Often we ask God to do things for us that we could easily do ourselves; and so God also has to teach us to help ourselves.

In the third play, both children did wrong. The boy did something he knew to be selfish and wrong, and the girl did wrong because she did not do something she knew would have been right. They both felt sorry afterwards, and said so; then they went away to do the right thing. We need to know, and admit, that we are wrong sometimes, so that we can put ourselves right. We need to say sorry to God, too.

Talking to God is just like talking to other people, really. He *does* hear our prayers; sometimes his answers are hard to hear, and to understand, but they are there, just the same.

Prayers
O God, hear us as we speak to you. We have been told that you are good and kind and loving. We have read about you, and talked *about* you, but until we actually talk *to* you we can never really know you. Help us, in our prayers, to feel that we are in touch with you, and that you are ready to guide us, and teach us, and give us courage. You will never let us down, Father God, we are sure, because you are waiting to be a true friend to each one of us.

After each part of this prayer allow a short pause before the words 'Listen to our thanks, O God'.
Let us think of one game we have enjoyed playing, and let us thank God for the strength of mind and body which makes us able to play it.
> Listen to our thanks, O God.
Let us think of one thing that we have made with our hands, and let us give thanks that we had the skill to make it.
> Listen to our thanks, O God.
Let us think of one book that we have enjoyed, and let us give thanks for being able to read it.
> Listen to our thanks, O God.
Let us think of just one new thing that we have learnt recently, and let us give thanks that we keep finding out more and more.
> Listen to our thanks, O God.
Let us think of one of the stories of Jesus, and let us give thanks that he lived and walked on this earth.
> Listen to our thanks, O God.

Hymns
Father, hear the prayer we offer
God be in my head
Our Father, who art in heaven   (CP 51)

Readings
Jesus came to tell us what God is like, and he also told us how to talk to God.
He said:

> 'When you say your prayers, don't babble away without thinking about
> what you are saying. That is what they are doing in temples all over the world;
> people think God listens to you if you just go on talking and talking. Don't do
> that sort of thing. You know what God is like: he is your Father, and he knows
> just what you need before you begin to ask him for it.'

(Matthew 6.7-8, NW)

Jesus gave us one very special prayer. His friends had asked him how they
should pray, and he answered them:

> 'Pray then like this:
> Our Father who are in heaven,
> Hallowed be thy name.
> Thy kingdom come,
> Thy will be done,
>   On earth as it is in heaven.
> Give us this day our daily bread;
> And forgive us our debts,
>   As we also have forgiven our debtors;
> And lead us not into temptation,
>   But deliver us from evil.'

(Matthew 6.9-13, RSV)

Follow-up for the class-room

1   Examine, and discuss, the different types of prayer: worship and praise,
thanks, admittance of wrongs and pleas for forgiveness, prayers for others
and ourselves, and prayers where nothing is said, but God is acknowledged
and meditated upon.

2   Make prayer books, either individual ones or ones that can be used in the class-room or in the Assembly, which incorporate the different types of prayer.

3   Younger or less able children: make wall posters with the general title of 'We talk to God'. (a) We praise him: pictures of the wonders of the world about us. (b) We thank him: pictures of food, clothing, shelter, and people who help us. (c) We ask him to care: pictures showing people in special need — refugees, starvation victims, those hurt by war, earthquake, flood etc (make this as topical as possible). When the sheets are finished use them as prayer guides in the class-room, or for the children to think about as they say their individual prayers at home.

4   Look at, and explain, the phraseology of the Lord's Prayer. Discuss its family implications, emphasising the ideal of brotherhood in each phrase. Relate each verse to life by short dramatic scenes, or by the stories of great Christian men and women through the ages. Look up the biblical words of the Lord's Prayer (Matthew 6.9-13; Luke 11.2-4), reminding the children that in early Christian days it was a fresh and meaningful prayer, as it still should be today. Perhaps a sung version could be learnt, or a record or cassette played of a choir singing the Lord's Prayer in an unfamiliar setting.

Instructions for today

The Assembly

Talk

This Assembly could be taken when a new school rule is introduced, or an old one needs reinforcing. If neither of these applies, begin the talk with questions and answers about rules being followed in games, such as football or rounders, and then go on to remind the children about some of the rules that have to be followed for the smooth running of the school.

Instructions are like rules; where can you find instructions? *(Encourage answers which might include: with model-making kits, with board or card games, in recipe books, in knitting patterns, on packets of seeds, etc)* These instructions are given to help us to use things properly or to do things the right way.

Some instructions are more like orders: 'Keep off the grass', 'Shut the gate', 'Danger, keep out', 'Cross now'. Can you think of any others? These instructions are given to keep people safe, or to protect people's property, just as the school rules are made for the safety and well-being of everyone here.

Have you ever taken part in a treasure hunt? Have you had to follow clues, or instructions, to find the treasure? It would take much longer to get to it if there were no instructions! Trying to follow Jesus is a bit like taking part in a treasure hunt: we are given some clues, or instructions, like 'Don't bully other people; be kind to them', 'Give help to those who need it', 'Share the good things you have' and 'Think of others first'. If you follow the instructions, or clues, you will become the sort of people who are needed in this world.

Alternative talk

If the leader wants children to take part in this Assembly, the rules (1) (Luke 10.27) and (2) (Luke 10.27) below could be read, either by individuals, or by groups; the reading (3) from Mark 3.1-5 could be presented in the same way.

In the days when Jesus was growing up his people were expected to live by

121

long sets of rules. Some of them were very good rules, like this one:

(1) Love the Lord your God with all your heart, with all your soul, with all your strength, and with all your mind.

And this one:

(2) Love your neighbour as you love yourself.

Many of these rules had been handed down for centuries. Moses had given the first ones to his people, telling them that they were from God. 'Respect your parents' said one of the laws, and 'Do not commit murder' was another, and 'Do not steal, or wrongly accuse another person'. All sensible, good rules. Moses expected his people to keep them, just as everyone here expects the school rules to be kept.

As the years went by, the leaders of the Jewish people added more rules to the ones Moses had given them. Some of them didn't really make much sense, and many of them were hard to follow. The Sabbath day, said the leaders, was a holy day, and should be kept as a day of rest. This, in itself, was a sensible law; everyone needed a day free from work, when he could worship and rest. But gradually the Sabbath day laws became more complicated. Nobody was allowed to work at all; all business and trading stopped; no work was done in the vineyards or in the fields, no housework was done, no fires lighted, no meals cooked.

Think what it would have been like. If you went out in the rain, or fell into a river, and all your clothes got soaking wet, your mother would not be allowed to light a fire to dry them. That was work. Or if your baby brother cried a lot on the Sabbath day, your father could not lift him and carry him about to soothe him. That was work. If you fell over and cut yourself your mother could put a bandage on to the wound so that it would not get any worse, but she would not be allowed to put ointment on it to make it get better. That was work.

Of course, there were difficulties when it came to things that could not be avoided, like making sure the sheep and cattle had water. You were allowed to lead the animals to the watering place, and you could draw water from the well and put it into the trough. But you were not allowed to carry the water to the animals. That was work. They must come forward to drink for themselves.

The trouble with these extra rules and instructions was that very few people could remember them all, and lots of people found them really inconvenient, so they began to think of ways of getting round them.

Jesus himself followed many of the rules and thought they were good. But sometimes he became impatient with them, and broke them.

This story tells of him in the synagogue, the house of God, on the Sabbath day:

(3) Then Jesus went back to the synagogue, where there was a man who had a paralysed hand. Some people were there who wanted to accuse Jesus of

doing wrong; so they watched him closely to see whether he would heal the man on the Sabbath. Jesus said to the man, 'Come up here to the front.' Then he asked the people, 'What does our Law allow us to do on the Sabbath? To help or to harm? To save a man's life or to destroy it?'

But they did not say a thing. Jesus was angry as he looked round at them, but at the same time he felt sorry for them, because they were so stubborn and wrong. Then he said to the man, 'Stretch out your hand.' He stretched it out, and it became well again. *(Mark 3.1-5, GNB)*

These days there are very few unnecessary laws, and the laws we have are there for very good reasons. Think about the Sabbath laws sometimes, and remember how lucky we are to have so few!

Readings

Here are some instructions which Jesus gave his friends. He wanted to make sure they would become the sort of people he, and the world, needed. About kind deeds he said:

'So when you give something to a needy person, do not make a big show of it, as the hypocrites do in the houses of worship and on the streets. They do it so that people will praise them. I assure you, they have already been paid in full. But when you help a needy person, do it in such a way that even your closest friend will not know about it. Then it will be a private matter. And your Father, who sees what you do in private, will reward you.'

About prayer he said:

'When you pray, do not use a lot of meaningless words, as the pagans do, who think that God will hear them because their prayers are long. Do not be like them. Your Father already knows what you need before you ask him.'

About worry he said:

'This is why I tell you not to be worried about the food and drink you need in order to stay alive, or about clothes for your body. After all, isn't life worth more than food? And isn't the body worth more than clothes? Look at the birds flying around: they do not sow seeds, gather a harvest and put it in barns; yet your Father in heaven takes care of them! Aren't you worth much more than birds? Can any of you live a bit longer by worrying about it?

'And why worry about clothes? Look how the wild flowers grow: they do not work or make clothes for themselves. But I tell you that not even King Solomon with all his wealth had clothes as beautiful as one of these flowers. It is God who clothes the wild grass — grass that is here today and gone tomorrow, burnt up in the oven. Won't he be all the more sure to clothe you?'

(Matthew 6.2-4, 7-8, 25-30, GNB)

123

Hymns
Fill thou my life, O Lord my God
God is working his purpose out
Reach out to your neighbour   (SM 22)

Prayer
Help us to follow your instructions gladly, Lord God, and to keep our eyes looking your way, that we may come at last to the full treasure of knowing and loving you for always.

Follow-up for the class-room

1   Make a list of school rules, home rules, and rules of the road and country. Examine together why they have been laid down.

2   Jesus once gave certain instructions to a man; read Luke 18.18-23. Make up an ending to the story; for example: what happened to the man? Did he ever give up his way of life and follow as a disciple?

3   Make a scroll and write on it the ten commandments of Moses, from Deuteronomy 5.6-21 or Exodus 20.1-17. Together make a rule that you think Christians should try to follow today.

Abbreviations and acknowledgements

The following abbreviations have been used in this book:

AV   Authorised Version
CP   Come and Praise
GNB   Good News Bible
NEB   New English Bible
NW   New World
RSV   Revised Standard Version
SM   Sing it in the Morning
WQ   Winding Quest

The author and publishers are grateful for permission to quote from the following Bible versions:

Good News Bible: © American Bible Society, New York 1976
New English Bible: © Oxford and Cambridge University Presses 1970
New World by Alan T. Dale: © Oxford University Press 1967
Revised Standard Version: © 1946 and 1962 Division of Christian Education, National Council of Churches of Christ in the USA
Winding Quest by Alan T. Dale: © Oxford University Press 1972

Bible readings

The following readings have been included in this book:

Mark 1.16-20	62
Mark 3.1-5	123
Mark 4.35-39	97
Mark 6.8-9	46
Mark 10.46-52	33
Mark 13.9-11a,13	26
Luke 1.28-33	36
Luke 10.25-37	30-31
Luke 10.27	122
Luke 10.38-42	62
Luke 14.16-23	13
Luke 15.11-20,22-24	92
Luke 17.3-4	76
Luke 19.1-8	51
Luke 20.9-15	75
Luke 23.23-24,32-34,44-46	75
Luke 23.32-34	56
John 8.12	64
John 20.19-20,24-29	79-80
Acts 1.3-4	109
Acts 2.1-4	109
Acts 3.1-8	108-109
Acts 8.4-13	59
Romans 4.21	15
Romans 12.4-8	113
Romans 15.13	94
1 Corinthians 13.1-7	91
2 Corinthians 11.26-27	46
Ephesians 4.22-24	52
2 Timothy 3.14-17	101-102
Hebrews 12.1-2a,3	26
James 2.14-18	113
1 John 1.5b-7a	66